ISLAM IS...

ISLAM IS...

Mary Margaret Funk

Lantern Books • New York
A Division of Booklight Inc.

2003
Lantern Books
A Division of Booklight Inc.
One Union Square West, Suite 201
New York, NY 10003
Copyright Sisters of Saint Benedict
of Beech Grove, Ind., Inc. 2003

Printed in the United States of America.

Library of Congress Cataloging-in-Publication Data

Funk, Mary Margaret.
Islam is : an experience of dialogue and devotion /
Sr. Mary Margaret Funk.
p. cm.
ISBN 1-59056-061-2 (alk. paper)
1. Islam. 2. Islam—Essence, genius, nature.
3. Islam—Relations—Christianity.
4. Christianity and other religions—Islam. I. Title.
BP161.3.F86 2003
297—dc21
2003011725

printed on 100% post-consumer waste paper, chlorine-free

Acknowledgments

I would like to acknowledge the following for their help on this book: Martin Rowe, Gene Gollogly, Sarah Gallogly, Dr. Shahid Athar, Dr. John Borelli, Dr. Sayyid M. Syeed, Katie Funk, Colleen Mathews, Mary Sue Freiberger, OSB, Carol Falkner, OSB and my community, Sharon Richardt, DC, William Skudlarek, OSB and MID Board, the Serra Club of Indianapolis, Jane Owens and Friends of Benedict.

Contents

INTRODUCTION

Our Experience in Dialogue

John Borelli, PhD

I have known Mary Margaret Funk, OSB, for the whole period that she has served as the Executive Director of Monastic Interreligious Dialogue (MID). When we first met, I believe her primary experience in interreligious dialogue followed her work in supporting the network of Catholic monastics dedicated to intermonastic dialogue, mainly with Buddhists but also with Hindus and Sufis. While intermonastic dialogue is by no means closed to those of us who are not monks and nuns, it has its special character. Monastics—whether Buddhist, Catholic, Hindu or other—are trained, or "formed," to live a routine of prayer, work, study and service to others. Thus, they share across their traditions certain experiences—rising early for prayer, regular meetings with a spiritual guide, using disciplines to effect spiritual growth, routines of communal religious life, and so forth. Those of us who are not monastics find these exchanges fascinating, but we leave and go home to our families and the routines of life outside monastic environments. For us, a monastic environment is a retreat

1

from the distractions of day-to-day life. The famous Trappist monastic of the twentieth century, Thomas Merton, was one of the most popular spiritual writers of his time, and he is viewed as one of the patron saints of inter-monastic dialogue. It was precisely as a monastic who is skilled in spiritual techniques that Sister Meg Funk joined the Midwest Dialogue of Catholics and Muslims.

The Midwest Dialogue is one of three regional dialogues that the U. S. Conference of Catholic Bishops (USCCB) co-sponsors with Islamic organizations and groups. While it was my idea to attempt the dialogues, I can take only a fraction of the credit for their success. The first Catholic bishop to serve as Episcopal Moderator for Interreligious Relations was, like Sister Meg, also a Benedictine monastic: Joseph J. Gerry, OSB, bishop of the Catholic diocese of Portland, Maine. Like a good monastic, once he had agreed to serve as the moderator, he signed up for a summer course on Islam offered at the Pontifical Institute for Arabic and Islamic Studies in Rome. He showed a willingness to study. He and I also met with the board of Monastic Interreligious Dialogue, and he learned from his fellow monastics their views of the dynamics and values of interreligious dialogue.

In the early 1990s, Bishop Gerry and I invited Catholics and Muslims active in Catholic–Muslim dialogue from all over the country to gather. They came under the joint sponsorship of the American Muslim Council and the USCCB from places as diverse as Los Angeles and Boston,

Detroit and Houston and Washington, DC. We had two meetings that were fruitful in building trust and establishing a rapport between representatives of our two communities in the United States. However, there were two principal difficulties in convening these national dialogues—time and money. Goodwill and hope were in abundance, but Islamic organizations could not afford the costs of travel and the staff time needed to prepare for such dialogues. The leadership wanted them to happen, but their priorities naturally involved networking the Muslim communities around the country, advocating for their concerns in the halls of the United States Government, maintaining communications with the news media, supporting local communities, and convening Muslims. Setting funds aside for a national interreligious dialogue with the Catholic Church was beyond the scope and means of most organizations.

I therefore began taking a series of trips to Indianapolis, where the Islamic Society of North America (ISNA) has its headquarters in the suburb of Plainfield, to meet with the archdiocesan ecumenical/interreligious officer and his Muslim friends. I already knew the ISNA's Executive Director, Dr. Sayyid M. Syeed, from his days in the Washington, DC., area, and, with the support of local Catholic and Muslim leaders, I proposed to him that the USCCB would come to Indianapolis to meet with ISNA. Together we developed the model for a regional dialogue. Bishop Gerry would recommend a Catholic bishop to serve as the Catholic co-chair who would preside at the meeting with Dr. Syeed. Staff from the USCCB and ISNA would plan the meeting; we would use local facilities, and invite Catholics and Muslims from cities within an easy commute of Indianapolis to attend.

Regional dialogues depend on support from Catholic and Muslim leadership in the states surrounding the meeting site. Usually the Catholic representative at a regional dialogue is the diocesan ecumenical/interreligious officer, and usually, but not always, the Muslim participant is the imam at a prominent mosque in the territory of that diocese. The Catholic and Muslim partners from a particular city or diocese are usually already friends, having cooperated in a number of local projects and initiatives. Regional dialogues also depend on good relations in the hosting environment so that Catholic and Muslim participants feel supported by their communities at the site of the meeting. Finally, the dialogue leaders identify certain scholars to do much of the work in presenting papers and preparing common statements. These arrangements require flexibility and openness. Currently, there are over forty Islamic leaders participating in three regional dialogues.

The first meeting of the Midwest Dialogue of Catholics and Muslims took place in 1996. The following year, Sister Meg came to an evening program in conjunction with the second meeting of the dialogue. By then, the members of the dialogue had decided to hold a series of meetings on the topic the word of God. We began discussing Jesus Christ, who is the Word of God made flesh for Christians, and God's guidance in divine words, which Muslims believe is the Qur'an. We also started some intertextual work, providing exegesis of passages of the New Testament and the Qur'an. By the third meeting, we wanted to compare how in each of our traditions the word of God is prayed, and I had asked Sister Meg to join us and speak on the practice of *lectio divina*—the meditative reading of scripture as a form of prayer. After her talk, which held our Muslim friends spellbound because of the depth of monastic tradition from which she drew in presenting this practice, Sister Meg was a regular participant in our dialogues.

After her presentation on *lectio divina*, Sister Meg was a welcomed member of the dialogue, and she has participated eloquently and attentively at the subsequent meetings. With Sister Meg's participation, the wife of a Muslim physician, who with her husband had been accompanying the office from the archdiocese of Louisville, also moved to the table. The archdiocese of Chicago always sends a female representative, and some of the women on staff at ISNA attend.

The subject of the role and rights of women in contemporary Islam and Muslim societies often surfaces in the form of questions and even challenges when Christians and Muslims meet in the United States. Most of the Catholic participants are priests, because the overwhelming majority of diocesan ecumenical/interreligious officers are

ordained. Yet the role, privileges, and exclusion of women
in both traditions are truly in evidence. In spite of the fact
that women have led democratic governments in some of
the most populous Muslim nations, the laws of the Taliban
and those imposed on Iran after the fall the Shah are more
often remembered. Mary, the mother of Jesus, is the only
woman mentioned by name in the Qur'an. Women in
Arabic-speaking societies after Muhammad were signifi-
cantly better off legally than they were before the time of
the Prophet. Mary Magdalen might very well have been the
first disciple to meet the risen Lord. Women are serving
greater leadership roles in contemporary Catholic Church
life than at any time in history. In many instances, women
serve leadership roles in Muslim communities today.

With Muslims breaking for prayer soon after noon, in
mid-afternoon, evening and at night, participants in our
dialogue are immersed in the style and form of Muslim
prayer. This involves the segregation of men and women.
The modesty of Muslim women is also very apparent in our
society, which seems to have no standard for public
modesty. At one meeting, a Muslim official asked that
sheets or tablecloths be draped over the meeting tables
arranged in a large rectangle so that our legs would not be
so evident. He said, "We are not dialoguing with our legs."
A Muslim woman at a Jewish–Christian–Muslim trilateral
dialogue which had both men and women equally in atten-
dance said that when she lives day to day in the United
States she wears a scarf, but when she goes home to

Lebanon she takes it off. In both instances, she says, she is making a point about the status and place of women in society and imagination. In the United States she does not want to be an object of sexual fantasy, and in Lebanon she does not want to be set off in the category of devout women who would never complain about a secondary role. I should add that she is a first-class professor of constitutional law.

When I am asked about women in Islam and in Muslim societies, I respond that we need to hear what Muslim women are saying among all the other voices who can respond to these questions. Muslims say to me that Catholic women need to be heard, too. We have an example of this in this book.

All our regional dialogues are retreats. If there is no spiritual dimension to our meetings, they are not interreligious dialogues. Catholics attend Muslim prayers and Muslims attend usually a morning or evening prayer service specially prepared for the occasion. The Catholics also celebrate Eucharist each morning. Our dialogues do not dwell on the past, since to focus only on history, whether positive or negative, and on traditional teaching is to avoid contemporary issues. There are so many facts from history and religious doctrine that can be brought into the discussion; however, the more important course in any dialogue is to let all the participants speak, men and women.

During this highly emotional time in the United States, with hostilities continuing in the Middle East, it is very difficult to bring together in a public way Jews, Muslims and Christians. It is no surprise that the successful cases are often women's groups, which often share common experiences and are, perhaps, better attuned to dialogue as a means to bridge differences. Besides all the political and religious questions that we Muslims and Christians bring to the table in dialogue, we also bring all the questions of significance in our lives. Parents gravitate toward other parents when the values of society are discussed. Citizens of the same land draw together in their assessments of questions in their society. College students share the same aspirations and feelings.

In a dialogue, participants listen and speak. Sometimes, a dialogue issues a report or a statement; sometimes, individual participants in a dialogue write about the proceedings. A report, whether agreed upon word for word by all participants or prepared by an individual, is only a glimpse into what happens in a dialogue. Many times, I am asked for permission to record one of our dialogues, and my impulse is emphatically to turn down such a request. When a dialogue is recorded it ceases to be a dialogue and becomes a public event wherein everything said is put under careful scrutiny. People need to be at ease and to experience the trust of a group, and then they can speak their minds. Sometimes we have to be candid with our partners in dialogue, and while candor is required for the sake of truth and charity, it works best within the confines of dialogue and not in the public arena. I have never heard a Catholic or another participant in a dialogue deny an important teaching of their tradition. In the official dialogues in which I participate, it just does not happen. I have heard participants in very respectful ways raise questions and express concerns while being faithful to the teachings of their traditions.

Our Midwest dialogue demonstrates how the two national sponsors can share the costs. ISNA provides meeting space, and the USCCB takes care of the cost of rooms at a local motel provided at a discount rate for ISNA's business. Meal costs are shared for food that is provided by a Muslim caterer. The Catholics attend evening prayer with the Muslims and hold a vespers afterwards. At the motel, the same room that has been used by the Muslims for early morning prayer is later used by the Catholics for Eucharist. Most participants absorb the cost of travel since many can come by car, and often together. Expenses for the scholars are paid by the two sponsors. Sharing the cost of a dialogue is an important ingredient. Dialogues should not be bought, but paid for. The fact that most participants are already participants in dialogues and Christian–Muslim relations ensures that the meetings go beyond introductory conversation. The Catholic and Muslim partners return to their home towns and cities with a renewed spirit of cooperation for promoting relations at home.

In 1998, two years after the Midwest Dialogue began in Indianapolis, the Mid-Atlantic regional dialogue between the Islamic Circle of North America (ICNA) and the USCCB held its first meeting. ICNA is headquartered in

Jamaica, Queens, New York. A Catholic bishop and a
representative of ICNA co-chaired the sessions. After an
initial meeting at a retreat house on Staten Island and the
second meeting at St. Charles Seminary in Philadelphia, the
dialogue settled into the routine of meeting at Immaculate
Conception Center, a facility owned by the diocese of
Brooklyn and located in Queens. It provides overnight
rooms and meeting space for very little cost. Some food is
catered from an Islamic kitchen. ICNA has its headquarters
nearby. This dialogue has focused on marriage and family.
We have discussed the laws of marriage, the ceremonies,
and family life. At our fourth meeting in 2001, we spent
one evening at the Islamic Center of Long Island in West-
bury, New York. There the participants attended evening
prayer and then listened to two presentations. The
following year we held a similar set of events at ICNA's
headquarters. Holding a public event in the community
and including a meal is a way for the Muslim participants
to share in the sponsorship of the cost of the dialogue.

A third regional dialogue meets in Orange in Orange
County, California, at the Center for Spiritual Development
in the diocese of Orange. It first met in 2000 with sponsorship shared between Sunni and Shiite Muslim leaders in
Southern California, who came together on a *sura* or advi-
sory council. A Catholic bishop co-chaired with a Sunni and
a Shiite imam and director of an Islamic center, both in the
Orange County area. This group settled on the spiritual
topic of surrender or obedience to God, and spirituality has

been the general subject of all of its four meetings, including the most recent in February 2003. As part of the cost-sharing, the Islamic Center of Orange County or the Islamic Education Center of Orange County hosts the group for an evening for prayer, a meal and presentations. Presentations at the meeting in 2001 by Archbishop Alexander Brunett of Seattle and Dr. Muzammil Siddiqi were published in the March 29, 2001 issue of *Origins*, the documentary service of Catholic News Service.

All three regional dialogues meet annually, in a retreat environment, over one or two days. Participants attend from Indianapolis, Detroit, Chicago, St. Louis, Louisville, Cleveland, Toledo, Fort Wayne, Lafayette, Brooklyn, New York, Rockville Centre, Buffalo, Newark, Trenton, Philadelphia, Harrisburg, Orange, San Diego, Los Angeles, San Francisco, San Jose, Sacramento and Seattle.

The first session is usually an opportunity to catch up on what has happened in the intervening year. Here the flexibility of a dialogue is tested, but there is no point in us coming together as friends and interreligious companions unless we hear what is really troubling us. Thus, our meetings after September 11, 2001 were extremely profound and touched all participants at the deepest levels of friendship and trust. Gradually, each of the dialogues took time out from the schedule to address questions of religion, scripture and violence. I have observed that conversation has become more probing and the insights more profound in our discussions. As the war on terrorism has unfolded, the intensity of our friendships and conversations has increased. These reflections by Sister Meg on our relationship in dialogue through the Midwest Dialogue constitute a lesson in growth. Each of us has learned a great deal about the other religious tradition and each has been blessed and touch by the experience of Catholic–Muslim dialogue. Sister Meg shows how dialogue is not an isolated activity but an aspect of the spiritual life. As we begin to develop a Christian spirituality for interreligious dialogue, which is a new activity for religious people on the scale that it is practiced today, the testimonies of those involved in these dialogues and who serve as spiritual guides and observers will nurture us and give us insight.

John Borelli is Associate Director for the Secretariat for Ecumenical and Interreligious Affairs at the U. S. Conference of Catholic Bishops. He has served at the Secretariat for sixteen years, staffing dialogues with Muslims, Buddhists, Hindus, Anglicans and Orthodox Christians among a number of other activities, including serving as liaison to Monastic Interreligious Dialogue. For twelve years he has been a consultor to the Vatican's Pontifical Council for Interreligious Dialogue. He and his wife Marianne have three children. Before moving to the Washington, DC area, they lived in the New York metropolitan area for seventeen years, where they each earned a doctorate and taught at various academic institutions.

⇥ 1 ⇤

An Unlikely Voice

I would be the first to admit that I am an unusual person to be offering my thoughts on Islam. I grew up in northern Indiana and lived on a farm that produced acres of corn as far as the eye could see. I went to Catholic boarding school at age thirteen, and then, at age seventeen, after high school graduation in 1961, I entered Our Lady of Grace monastery in Indiana.[1] In 1994, I assumed the role of Executive Director for Monastic Interreligious Dialogue (MID). This group, consisting mostly of monastics, sponsors formal interreligious dialogues—mainly with Asian religions that have a monastic component.[2] I was two years into my role as Executive Director when I first met Islam. For seven years, I have participated in a series of formal Muslim–Catholic dialogues sponsored by the United States Conference of Catholic Bishops. Each year we have met in Indianapolis or the adjacent town of Plainfield, where we have been hosted by Dr. Sayyid M. Syeed of the Islamic Society of North America.

In spite of my personal commitment to dialogue, and even though we have had several thousand guests each year who have visited us at our retreat and conference center, Benedict Inn, and have hundreds of guests at the monastery itself, I do not recall that we have ever welcomed any Muslims for dinner in our refectory. We must prepare for this hospitality. This book, therefore, is my food for thought, my gift of welcome for my Muslim brothers and sisters. It is also my offer of introduction to Islam for the brothers and sisters of my own faith, and for all Christians who seek to understand Islam and its billion devotees throughout the world.

This book is written from the perspective of someone who has spent every day of the seven years of Muslim–Catholic dialogue in dialogue with and practicing her own faith. As a Benedictine nun, I have studied the origin of our monastic order in the sixth century and see the value of grasping the spiritual life as envisioned by the founder of our order, St. Benedict (c.480–c.547). I am grateful for the opportunity to look at Islam as I would look at Benedict's teaching. What is the way of life that both were imparting? What do St. Benedict and Muhammad embody for their followers?

For Christians, Jesus Christ is the Son of God, and the Qur'an holds him up as a great prophet—Muslims believe that Jesus was born miraculously and that he performed many miracles. While there are, clearly, substantial doctrinal differences between Christianity and Islam, there are, nonetheless, parallels. Muslims have the same relationship to the Qur'an as the word of God as Christians do to

Christ, the Word of God. On a more personal level, because I follow the Rule of St. Benedict, I know how it feels to revere a human founder and to follow that human founder's path. Even though we know little about the historical Benedict, we nevertheless have a Rule that was written by him and clearly teaches the monastic way of life. Both Muslims and Benedictines, therefore, recognize that historical biography cannot explain fully the call to follow a practice.

This is why it is my belief that to understand Islam we must, as it were, "get underneath" the genius of Muhammad and see how Islam embodies the message he received from God as it has manifested itself in the lives of my Muslim friends attempting to live that message. Historical fact and biography aside, all I truly "know" about Islam from my own experience is what I see embodied in the Muslims at the table of dialogue. The challenge for me is to live my Christian way of life in such a way that my Muslim friends "catch" the spirit of Christ just as I believe I have "caught" their Muslim way of life. It is thus in this spirit that I set out my understanding of Islam—I have received the beauty of this noble path and hope to convey that beauty to you.

While I am sure that I will never comprehend Islam as a member of that family of faith would, I feel that my warm experience, such as it is, has allowed me to "meet" the faith with honesty and humility. In the pages that follow I intend to share my "meeting" with the profoundly complex and sacred tradition of Islam. We who call ourselves Christians are at a turning point in our relationship with Muslims in our shared world. The wars in Afghanistan and Iraq, and the effort of the international community to combat terrorism, all require us to look deeply into the heart of Islam and its faith, its plurality of cultures and civilization. If we do not, we miss a jewel in our midst and risk generations upon generations of conflict because of ignorance.

Not only do I write as someone who is a practitioner and has been involved in interreligious dialogue with Buddhists and Hindus, I also write as a woman. As a woman, I have come to understand that women religious face unique challenges within their respective traditions. Catholic women religious face some common issues with Muslim women—from obtaining recognition as religious leaders to having the right even to speak and be respected as equals. My approach, however, has been neither to confront nor to walk away. It has been helpful for me to ask questions and, more importantly, to listen and try to make sense of what I see rather than simply stand back and observe. I have also sought to reclaim women's roles wherever it is possible. In this, I am not an advocate so much as a woman who simply practices her faith to the fullest extent of my capabilities. When I was the superior of my monastic community I performed my role alongside the ordained chaplain. In some ways, it would be taking the easy option to sit back and complain that I cannot preside at Eucharist, and choose to refuse to preside over the rituals that a non-ordained woman may conduct without further permission from a bishop. Instead of focusing on what I cannot do, however, I have done what I can. In the dialogue with my Muslim friends, I do the same thing. In this way, I am at the table and engaged, and I have experienced being heard by my male dialogue partners at the meetings. However, this has been a challenge. In the first two years of the Muslim–Catholic dialogue I was the only woman. Now there are other women more competent than I, such as Sister Joan McGuire from the archdiocese of Chicago, who are engaged in the dialogue, and this delights me. We are in this dialogue together.

The biggest misconception that has greeted me in the seven years of Muslim–Catholic dialogue has been the thought that my belief in Jesus the Son of God and the Trinity would be a barrier to our further understanding of one another, since Muslims see the Qur'an and not Jesus as the Word of God. However, I have been pleased and awestruck at my Muslim dialogue partners' connection with and consciousness of God—the same God I love and obey—whom I call God the Father and whom they call God with no Second. Therefore, while Muslims differ from Catholics, without a doubt we can affirm one another in our way of life under this same God that transcends all of us.

I have discovered that when you are in dialogue, an amazing phenomenon occurs: you share your faith and listen respectfully as the Buddhist, Hindu, Taoist or Muslim shares his or her heart's desire. What happens is that you begin to "feel" that what they are experiencing is the same as what you feel in your own heart. There is no need to correct one another's view; instead, there is a real and mutual acceptance of each other's way. You acknowledge to yourself that while their way may not be your way, you are bearing witness to the integrity of their way and it feels sound, good and true. This may seem counterintuitive—after all, so many of our religious traditions have doctrinal distinctions that sometimes appear to make dialogue impossible. Nevertheless, it is my experience that one's differences need not divide. Our differences are real, and those differences are not merely nothing to worry about; instead, they are worth celebrating, because they are the truth!

In the flash of time that these years of dialogue represent, my faith has grown deeper because of dialogue. I have found real friendship—a friendship not of submerged identities but one where our unique and distinct religions emerge. We can even promote the "other" religion while being wholly faithful to our own. The Buddhist scholar Joseph Goldstein talks about "not knowing" as a respectful way of letting two views live side by side. I feel that the practice of dialogue is one of "not knowing." That said, from the inside it feels like I "know" how that religion feels for me. It seems that in deepest dialogue in friendship with each other we share the same dimension of the one, true and universal experience of the holy. Indeed, whenever we become overly "literal" in the interpretation of our faith and insist on a linear logic to express it, the mystery that holds so much of our religious practice and feelings is diminished.

During these years, I have entered through the doors of the world's sacred scriptures with awe and trembling. I have sought as much as possible to put aside preconceptions and prejudices and opened my heart to receive those scriptures reverently and apprehend what grace makes present for me. As I have said, I have no illusion that I will come to a full understanding or see into that scripture's revelations. Instead, I bow as deeply as I can and then return to my own Christian scriptures for the revelation of God that resonates with my baptismal initiation and monastic vows.

My dialogue partner in this book is Shahid Athar, MD, whom I have asked to comment on this text in an afterword. I welcome his wisdom, wit and passion for truth, and hope that one day he will write his own "take" on Catholics. In my years of East–West dialogue, I have always taken the position of letting the "other" define him- or herself and not feel the need to speak for them. It is out of respect for this that I have listened these last seven years to my Muslim friends. Indeed, this little book was prompted by an event of dialogue, a routine Monday noon luncheon meeting with Serra Club International (an organization set up to help those preparing for priesthood and the vocational life) at the Southside (Indianapolis) Knights of Columbus Hall. I asked three Muslim friends to speak, and each respectfully declined as they had work obligations. So I spoke on Islam myself, and the response was overwhelming. My Catholic friends were amazed and inspired; they had questions beyond my capacity to answer. Because the dialogue continues, I see the need for little books such as this one.

There are 1.2 billion Muslims, one billion Catholics, and 500 million other Christians who share our planet. It seems to me that the two dominant religions should have a "feel" for one another—since religion is in service for all of us humans on Earth. If this book gives you something of that "feel," then it might lead to a relaxation of tensions and a move toward peace.

Notes

1. Our Lady of Grace Monastery was founded in 1961 in Ferdinand, Indiana. This Benedictine Monastery has eighty-five nuns and sponsors St. Paul Hermitage, a retirement facility for lay elderly, and Benedict Inn, a retreat and Conference Center. The monastery is now located in Beech Grove, near Indianapolis. Our Lady of Grace Monastery can be contacted via the Web, at www.benedictine.com, or email: olgmonastery@aol.com.

2. MID was established in 1978 at the request of the Congress of Abbots and is accountable to the Vatican's Pontifical Council of Interreligious Dialogue under the General Secretary Pierre de Bethune of MID and its European branch, DIM. MID/DIM publishes a MID Bulletin twice a year. Its Web site, www.monastic-dialog.com, provides extensive coverage of our current work and previous accomplishments.

⊰ 2 ⊱

An Earthly Religion

During my graduate days at the Catholic University of America, I was taught the social sciences alongside my theological studies. This approach presents religion as a human craft, and teaches that God's revelation comes through the human voice in the context of the human condition. It shows us that religions have the brilliance of human institutions and the foibles of human mistakes and proclivities. There are many religions: Hinduism, Jainism, Sikhism, Confucianism, Zoroastrianism, Judaism, Christianity, Buddhism, Islam, to name the major rivers that have carried millions of peoples over time to their destinations. Yet it has been my experience that most members of a religion do not like to be completely bracketed in a particular religion, because that religion never names the full experience of being a devotee, an adherent, a disciple, a practitioner or a believer. Religion, in short, is a name from the outside.

As students of religion, we made a distinction between religion on the one side and Christianity on the other. "Religion" was the word we used for the cultural phenomenon, and—for us—Christianity was the "way of

Christ." Catholicism is a particular form of the way to follow Christ. Even though this distinction offers an overly simple view of the world, I have nevertheless found it helpful to separate the human shortfalls from the sublime revelation.

In 1995, several of us involved in Monastic Interreligious Dialogue made a journey to northern India and Tibet. His Holiness the Dalai Lama invited us to take part in a formal dialogue with members of the five lineages of Tibetan Buddhism. Eager to learn about their religion and the distinctions between their schools, we asked some of the Tibetans how their particular form of Buddhism differed from Zen Buddhism, as practiced in Japan, and Theravada Buddhism, as practiced in Southeast Asia. Our question, however, turned out to be a non-question: we knew more "about" Buddhism than these practitioners did. They had no feel for what we might call the *landscape* of Buddhist practice; since they knew their own practice from the inside, they felt there was no need to survey the field of Buddhism as if they were observers. It was a humbling moment of recognition for all of us who seek to understand other religions. Those of us who study religions as well as those who are involved in interreligious dialogue soon find out that all talk is "outside" the experience.

A similar point was made to me by Dr. Thubten Norbu, the Dalai Lama's oldest brother. He told me that there was no such thing as Buddhism, only decent human beings. He was reminding me not to get caught up in the doctrinal distinctions and formalism of religion. That said, I feel that it helps to know the "family origins" of each religious practitioner, since I believe that such knowledge helps us to create and live in a society where pluralism flourishes. However, it is always people, not the religion, who matter.

* * *

Islam is a religion and a follower of Islam is a Muslim. A Muslim believes in the revelation of God through the Qur'an which was given to the most holy prophet, Muhammad (570–632). In Christianity, the revelation was the incarnation of Jesus Christ, and the followers then wrote the story of Jesus' words and deeds in an inspired text. For a Muslim, the Qur'an is God's Word. This word was memorized and recited by professional memorizers during the lifetime of Muhammad and then written down in classical Arabic about two decades after Muhammad's death. In my opinion, the key to understanding Islam is to "know" this prophet and respect the Qur'an as Islam's authentic revelation. It is important to take seriously what are known as the five pillars of Islam and to comprehend how effective they are in forming a people of God. Lastly, it is necessary to weave together a few main threads that bind the Muslim faith into an intelligible whole. These themes, which I will explore later on in this book, are as follows:

- The cultural context of the desert and Islam as a civilization
- The cohesiveness of the word/observance/unmediated symbol system
- The beliefs in God's blessings through economic prosperity
- The notion of ascendancy that comes about through the belief that previous revelations in Judaism or Christianity have been fulfilled in Islam.

It is important to understand what Islam is *not*. Islam does not have a monastic tradition. We monks and nuns live in an alternative culture that ritualizes all our work and prayer. Islam uses the world as its full stage and theater. There is no separation between the visible and invisible, the physical and the spiritual dimensions.

There are orders of people called Sufis, named after the woolen cloths that they originally wore to set them apart, who practice a kind of Islamic mysticism in which they cultivate a direct and personal experience of God. Nevertheless, Sufis have never separated themselves out from ordinary family life and the marketplace, though they have an alternative "family," as in our Benedictine cenobitic or monastic tradition. According to my Hindu teacher, with whom I studied for five years, Sufis in India could be Hindu rather than Muslim and their expression of faith pre-dated Islam in origin. Later, their guru was a sheikh of Islam. Orders of Sufis with a lineage of enlightened sheikhs flourished throughout the Muslim world from the eighth and ninth centuries to the present day.

Islam also has no priesthood. It has no unifying leader such as the Pope—although the question of leadership within Islam has been an issue of contentious division between the two major branches of Islam, Sunni and Shia. There is also no universal or authoritative way to speak for the tradition. There is no single doctrinal council of teachers, nor is there a system of provinces and dioceses, parishes and congregations, such as you find in the vast world of Christianity. Islam is an earthly religion that functions more like a civilization with many diverse cultures that keeps its face directly turned to the One God. There is no Church to mediate it. The sacraments—if one looks for a parallel system with Christianity—consist of the Qur'an and ordinary life's blessings of family and prosperity. There is no ritual table of Eucharist where the word (the bread) is broken and community is gathered. For Muslims community is actual and not symbolic. Christians recall Christ's death on the cross ritually at Eucharist, symbolically through gesture and in eating bread and drinking wine, remembering Christ at the Altar of Sacrifice. Professor Ewert Cousins suggests that when Shiite men beat their chests in grief at the martyrdom of Imam Hussein, grandson of the Prophet Muhammad, in the solemn festival of Muharram, it reflects a similar and ancient impulse to sacrifice oneself as one's leader was in turn sacrificed.

I will begin by looking at the life of Muhammad.

Who Was Muhammad?

Muslims do not believe that the Holy Prophet Muhammad was an incarnation of God, nor do they, like Christians, believe that Jesus was the Son of God and an indivisible part of God. Muslims believe that Muhammad was a man and that he followed Adam, Abraham, Moses, David, Solomon and Jesus as the last of the great prophets to receive divine revelation.

Muhammad was born in Mecca (in what is now Saudi Arabia) in 570, and his early childhood was marked by loss. Muhammad's father Abdullah died before he was born, and his paternal grandfather, Abdul Muttalib, assumed responsibility for his upbringing. Then his mother Aminah died when he was six, and his grandfather died two years later. When Muhammad grew up, he became a merchant, traveling as far as Yemen and Syria with his uncle, Abu Talib. On these long journeys, Muhammad mixed with Christians and Jews and was attracted to the notion of the One God. He felt keenly that the Arabians, who worshiped many gods at that time, were bereft of a calling to the One God.

Muhammad was also acutely aware of the unjust distribution of wealth and the plight of the poor—the masses of people who had no access to the necessities of food, clothing and shelter in the harsh climate of the desert where everything was scarce. Mecca was a major trading center, with goods moving between Yemen and the Mediterranean regions of Gaza and Damascus. While the town was prosperous, Muhammad saw how the money was concentrated in only a few hands and how tribal divisions and individual greed not only threatened the stability of the clans and tribes but also impeded the traditional Arab custom of helping the poor.

When Muhammad was forty years old and undergoing his period of solitude in the mountains (as was a practice of the devout in his time) he experienced a profoundly life-changing mystical experience. Through the mediation of the angel Gabriel, Muhammad received the first in a series of revelations, which came to him over a period of twenty years. He shared these with his cousin Ali and his beloved wife Khadijah, whom he had married when he was twenty-four years old and who was sixteen years his senior. They encouraged him to speak more widely of what he saw and to recite the inspired vision to others.

Muhammad was a respected merchant but could neither read nor write. This point is critical in understanding his shock at this transcendent event. Muhammad tested the authenticity of his revelations with prayer and fasting, and it was two years before he went public with his profound religious experience. Those who heard him were caught up in his enthusiasm and the truthfulness of the transmission, which came in full, poetic, graceful Arabic that was beyond his personal capacity to compose or contrive. (Christians will recall Christ's disciples at Pentecost, when the rural fishermen were touched by flame and began speaking in tongues and with an eloquence that astonished the crowd who listened.) Muhammad spoke with conviction of Allah, the One God, and told his listeners that he had profoundly surrendered to Allah. From this came Muhammad's powerful understanding that, after one experiences God, it is impossible to do anything than simply and totally "surrender"—the literal meaning of the word *islam*.

Muhammad was awestruck by his revelations. He thought and felt like he was a prophet, such as those in the Hebrew scriptures and like Jesus in the Christian story, except he felt no claim to be Son of God, only a messenger. From what he knew from his travels of the lineage of the Jews and Christians, they were like him descendants of Abraham. Over time, he understood his vocation to welcome the Arabian peoples to return to Abraham's God. However, he met with a number of reverses. He was surprised to find out that the Jews did not accept another prophet for another people. Furthermore, there was opposition to the recitations, as the verses Muhammad spoke were called, from the rich merchant class in Mecca. They felt threatened by his criticism of their lives and his increasing influence among the Arabs, whom he was beginning to gather to follow his leadership. The merchants began to undermine Muhammad.

After the death of Khadijah and his uncle in 619, Muhammad lost the support of another uncle, Abu Lahab, who withdrew protection from him and left him exposed to personal attacks. Muhammad then left Mecca, ending up in the nearby town of Medina. Muhammad's flight from Mecca is called the *hijrah* or "emigration." It is from this moment that the official Muslim calendar begins.

The move to Medina initiated a new phase in Muhammad's life. In Medina, Muhammad began to set in motion the ways of life that would lead to the surrender to God. These were: the worship of Allah three times a day (a practice that was later extended to five times), sharing wealth with the poor, reciting the Qur'an, fasting, and proclaiming the central doctrine of Islamic faith: "There is no God but God, and Muhammad is His messenger." These are called the five pillars of Islam. This orderly way of life, under a unifying God (Allah), was particularly attractive to the Bedouin tribes who lived around the region, and it was soon taken up by more and more desert dwellers and merchants in exchange for the safety that they got by gathering as a cohesive unit. Like many other groups in the region at the time, Muhammad's followers engaged in raids (*razzias*) on caravans as a way of redistributing wealth. As harsh though these raids seem to us now, they were an expected hazard for those who lived in and made their passage through the desert. Indeed, the defense against attack and attacking vans themselves seem to have been part of the ordinary rhythm of life at the time.

At first, Muhammad was gentle in his approach and nonviolent even with his enemies, especially those based in Mecca who by now felt very threatened by the power base that Muhammad had built for himself in Medina. After some years of loss and victory in battle on both sides, the turning point in Muhammad's fortunes occurred in 627, where the Meccans laid siege to Muhammad's followers near Medina. Even though the Meccans had promised to destroy Muhammad, they failed to dislodge his forces. This success fueled Muhammad's confidence and was seen by him and others as a sign of Allah's favor. Muhammad continued to preach Islam to Meccans with fervor. At last, he entered Mecca in triumph in 630.

The shift of consciousness that occurred with Muhammad's success and earthly prosperity and the solidarity felt by the followers of the new religion allowed the development of a community of believers, called an *umma*. Under God, these tribes and clans transcended their territorial and family boundaries and consolidated their possessions, family ties and identifying characteristics. In this way, Muslims envisioned the religion of Islam. God was the center, Muhammad was the leader, and the Qur'an was the Word of God from which all Muslims could find sustenance.

In the last years of Muhammad's life and shortly after his death in 632, Islam spread with lightning speed throughout the Middle East—borne on the wings of Muhammad's consolidation of Arabian tribes under Islam and his rapid rise to preeminence in the region. After the Persian Empire defeated the Byzantine Empire in 628, minority tribes in Yemen and other parts of Arabia, who had been under Byzantine security, turned to Muhammad for protection and converted to Islam. In 630, Muhammad took his followers on a campaign that reached the borders of Syria, an event that brought him into conflict with Christians. Between 634 and 650 Muslim forces routed Byzantine and Persian armies and took control of Libya, Egypt, Palestine, Syria, Iraq and most of modern-day Iran (Persia).[1] By the end of the eighth century, Islam had reached central Asia and India and had spread across Mediterranean Africa and into Spain and France, where its spread was halted at the Battle of Poitiers in 732.

Muhammad's death was sudden, and there was no obvious successor to take his place as temporal and spiritual leader of the Arabs. The resulting instability led to many years of struggle and dissension among his followers—particularly between those who followed Muhammad's son-in-law Ali (known as Shiites) and those who wished another follower, Abu Bakr, to be leader. (Abu Bakr lived for only two years after Muhammad's death and was followed as caliph—which literally means "deputy of the prophet"—by Umar and Uthman. It was this branch of Islam that became known as Sunni.) Such dissension became common as the Arabs extended their empire over an increasingly large geographic area, encompassing many different ethnic groups and cultural practices. Indeed, the rise of Shia Islam in the 640s was a response to the increasing worldliness of Sunni Islam as it took over the Persian Empire and made inroads into the Byzantine Empire. It is worth noting at this point that Caliph Umar pledged protection of the Jews when his forces took

Jerusalem in 641, and that it was the Christian Bishop of Egypt who invited the Muslims to enter his country to displace the Romans.

The Character of Muhammad

So, who was Muhammad? According to the early twentieth-century English biographer, Stanley Lane-Poole, Muhammad

> was of the middle height, rather thin, but broad of shoulders, wide of chest, strong of bone and muscle. His head was massive, strongly developed. Dark hair, slightly curled, flowed in a dense mass down almost to his shoulders. Even in advanced age it was sprinkled by only about twenty grey hairs. . . . His face was oval-shaped. . . . Fine, long, arched eyebrows were divided by a vein which throbbed visibly in moments of passion. Great black restless eyes shone out from under long, heavy eyelashes. His nose was large, slightly aquiline. His teeth upon which he bestowed great care were well set, dazzling white. . . . A full beard framed his manly face. His skin was clear and soft, his complexion "red and white," his hands were as "silk and satin.". . . His step was quick and elastic, yet firm, and as that of one "who steps from a high to a low place." In turning his face he would also turn his full body. His whole gait and presence were

dignified and imposing. His countenance was mild and pensive. His laugh was rarely more than a smile.[2]

Beyond this physical description, we know that Muhammad was a saintly man. He had seven children: three sons who died at birth and four daughters who also died young. Only Muhammad's daughter Fatima was living at the time of his death. He was devoted to his first wife Khadijah until her death, although he later had other wives, as was the custom at the time. Reports show him to be very charismatic, fast-speaking, but prone to silence. He was vigorous and yet gentle, especially with children. Although he had much success on the battlefield, he lived more like an ascetic than a general or imperial ruler. He counseled measured action in response to adversity. Although by nature solitary, he nonetheless was very involved in the life of the community and his family, apart from the month of Ramadan. More than anything else, however, he seemed totally engaged in his relationship with God.[3]

Muhammad was a prophet, a visionary, a family man who had children, and a political and religious leader who pulled together many clans and followers to surrender before the One God, Allah. He transmitted a sense of awe to a family of believers under the One God who would protect, guide and bring them to the promised life in the next world but also bless them abundantly in this earthly life. A Muslim would say that Muhammad's greatest contribution to the world was to mediate the word of God that we know today as the Qur'an—the central scripture that proclaims that Allah is One for 1.2 billion Muslims around the world and holds communities from Jakarta to Lahore and Indianapolis to Cape Town together.

Notes

1. James Harpur, *The Atlas of Sacred Places: Meeting Points of Heaven and Earth*. (New York: Henry Holt & Co., 1994), pp. 208–9.
2. Quoted in *The Benefactor* by Fakir Syed Waheeduddin (Chicago: Kazi Publications, 1961).
3. "Muhammad." *Encyclopædia Britannica* 2003. Encyclopædia Britannica Premium Service, March 23, 2003 <http://www.britannica.com/eb/article?eu=108142>.

⊰ 3 ⊱

The Pillars of Islam

1. The Profession of Faith

As indicated earlier, there are five pillars to Islam. The first
pillar is the Muslims' ultimate profession of their faith, the
shahada: *la ilaha illa Allah; Muhammad rasul Allah*,
"There is no god but Allah, and Muhammad is the prophet
of Allah." This confession is repeated at least five times
each day by the *muezzin* in the minaret of every mosque
around the world as an invitation to prayer. Just as it is
impossible to exaggerate the importance of the Qur'an for
a devout Muslim, so it would be hard to exaggerate how
central this first pillar of belief is. The belief in the one,
transcendent God is the pole around which the whole religion orbits. Muslims believe in a dualistic universe: there is
an "other," and that "other" is the created person or thing,
distinct from, but in relationship with, the One God. This
dualistic dynamic sets up the proper response to the God
who created the creature. God is transcendent and full of
mystery and in every dimension. There is no other like
God, no modifier. God, simply, is God.

While Islam traditionally lists ninety-nine names that
praise and glorify God, revealing some of God's character-

istics (the subtle, the nourisher, the watcher, the originator,
etc.), Christians need to understand that there is no possibility of division or distinction, as there is in the Christian
notion of the Trinity, or in the idea of Christ, whom Christians to be consider both God and human. In Islam there
are no exceptions to the indivisibility of the notion and
facticity of God and His Oneness. Notice that there are
two distinctions here that differ from the Christian notion
of God: first, God is One, not Trinity, and secondly, this
oneness conversely shows that any differentials would
diminish God as God, so God's One-ness is what it means
to be God. Nevertheless, in spite of these deep doctrinal
differences with Christianity, all Muslims honor the
monotheistic traditions of Christianity and Judaism
because we worship the One God. We are all "people of
the book," a testament to the respect that Islam has not
only for scholarship but also for the wisdom contained in
the Hebrew and Christian scriptures.

The transcendence of God is the dominant belief for a
Muslim. No image, doctrine or dogmas can postulate the
reality. The recognition of this transcendence is sacred
enough to cause the complete and total surrender of a creature. This was the main message of Muhammad, who saw
himself as reminding all peoples of the reality of God's
transcendence. Muhammad argued that the old patterns of
the old gods could not protect anyone, only Allah could.
The attractiveness of such a doctrine at that time and place
was clear—spiritual malaise and constant and destructive

internecine strife that violated all the tribal codes and traditions of Arabia made the clarity and compassion of the all-merciful God attractive. Henceforth, all Muslims were part of an increasingly global community, *umma*, which was governed by justice and equity.[1] The surrender implicit in the *shahada* is not just assented to notionally but is actually observed by the Muslim through the other four pillars of Islam. The personal and individual human's surrender is the way of salvation. There is no mercy through a human savior; every person must bend his will and lift up his mind in assent to God's transcendence, and God will reward the adherent with mercy and a life hereafter. One is a Muslim to the extent one appropriates the God-consciousness of Allah. There is no baptism or membership without practice. The five pillars literally sustain the faith.

This practice is not unlike a Christian's way of ceaseless prayer (1 Thessalonians 5:17). The mantra of *shahada* echoes in the heart and mind. It is a form of concentration, focus and total approbation. It does not concern itself with being *about* something. It is neither speculative nor philosophical in orientation. Instead, the *shahada* plunges through levels and levels of consciousness to penetrate the core of one's heart in a way of belief that is linked with prayer and pure moral conduct. With a clear mind one can make poised, thoughtful choices, provided with a constant awareness of God that is nourished with routine, daily and prescribed prayer.

2. Prayer

The second pillar of Islam is prayer (*salaat*), which is carried out five times a day: at dawn, noon, mid-afternoon, sunset, and after the fall of darkness or at bedtime. The actual prayers are accompanied by ritual cleansing, hand gestures, body bows and prostrations, and prescribed rubrics that apply whether you praying alone or with others.

I have personally seen this act of prayer many times. At the mosque in Plainfield, Indiana, women can watch the prayers and join from the back as the men line up and do the prayer with utmost devotion and precision. Each man prepares for the prayer through a ritual of ablution. They stand reverently in a straight line, offering certain prayers, bowing toward Mecca with hands on knees. They do not so much as offer Allah petitions, as Christians might think of prayers, but rather ascriptions of praise and declarations of submission to His holy will. The devotees straighten up, still praising Allah, then fall prostrate, kneeling with head to the ground, glorifying God. They then sit up reverentially and offer a petition. Finally, they bow again. Throughout this practice, the sacred sentence *Allahu akbar* ("God is great") is repeated again and again. It is common at the beginning simply to repeat the *fatiha*, which consists of the first words of the first *sura* of the Qur'an. Christians might consider this to be the equivalent of the Lord's Prayer:

Praise belongs to God, the Lord of all Being,
the All-merciful, the All-compassionate,
the Master of the Day of Doom.
Thee only we serve, to Thee alone we pray for
  succor.

Guide us in the straight path,
The path of those whom Thou hast blessed,
Not of those against whom Thou are wrathful,
Nor of those who are astray.[2]

Sometimes, usually on Friday at noon, one of the men stands before the devotees and offers words of inspiration. It is essential for Muslims to make the ground of prayer holy. On one occasion, when our Catholic–Muslim dialogue was taking place at Fatima Retreat House in Indianapolis, my Muslim colleagues insisted that the facility provide sheets to stand on so that they could make the floor a holy ground. I know individuals who travel with their own prayer rug to roll out for their *salaat* wherever they are. Once, while I was waiting at Chicago's O'Hare airport to catch a flight, I walked into the chapel and was surprised to see more Muslims than Christians saying midday prayers. At another interreligious dialogue event in Chicago, I visited a mosque and sat with the other women behind an ornate screen as prayers were conducted.

The fact that Muslims pray five times a day is dear to
my heart since, as a Benedictine nun, I too pray five times
a day. Our Divine Office is morning, noon and evening,
with mass and night prayers. I have witnessed and participated in the same prayer rhythm at Buddhist and Hindu
monasteries. Clearly, what is common to all these religions
is a human desire to sanctify the hours in an orderly way.
It is a way for us to recognize that if there is a God then we
must turn to God and bow. In the Buddhist traditions, of
course, practitioners bow not to God but to Buddha-nature
or the deities that share the realm of Clear Light.

The practice of regular prayer throughout the day gives
to time nothing more nor less than *graciousness*. The practice turns time inside out. What in my early years of
monastic life was an interruption to my day (all that stopping for prayers and starting again) turned into a ceaseless
and seamless way of being in time. For Benedictines, prayer
is itself embodied in work. We pray without ceasing. And
there is, undoubtedly, strength in numbers—about being
called to gather in a particular place to pray together. It is
easier for our practice if, at the beginning, middle and end
of the day and sometimes in between, we join with other
like-minded souls.

Morning, noon and night offer a natural impulse of the
human spirit to rise and give praise. When I was present for
the Muslim *salaat*, I felt as though I was at home with my
nuns in Beech Grove, Indiana. It was the same God, the
same praise and the same bended knee. This is why, as a

gesture of solidarity with my Muslim friends, every morning after a twenty-minute sit in the oratory I bow my forehead to the floor. I am not sure I am pointing toward any city here on Earth, let alone Mecca, as I sometimes sit in a different seat in the oratory. However, I am sure it is the same God to whom Muslims and Catholics alike direct our hearts.

The other similarity that exists between the religions in this regular kind of daily short prayer is the humility such practice requires. When the call to prayer is made you have to stop what you are doing and go to chapel or the mosque. There is no fudging or promising to pray twice as hard later. You have to leave your computer, your hoe or your basket. There is a higher power that rightfully claims your time, over and over again, commanding you to acknowledge your submission and allowing you to respond "yes" over and over again to that demand: "God is God and I obey." This is a right relationship.

Although we Benedictines and Muslims practice prayer as a form of worship, it is the practice in humility that makes it more readily possible to cease and desist doing our will when we should refrain and act on behalf of the other. This makes our aspiration an actual behavioral practice of moving from my self-centeredness toward another. The daily prayer practice provides me with the energy to give my goods as well as my time. Islam is an ingenious system of such energy direction—creating a spiritual *economy* (literally "the law of the home") not so much in the life hereafter (as in the salvation of Jesus Christ) but right now on Earth. For me, the benefit of all the prescribed prayer times is to secure the ceaseless prayer as a firm practice. I don't get far from prayer in my mind and heart; instead, I return to it over and over again. When I go through dry periods, my mind might wander during prayer; but my body is there and I do the rituals with exact form. Eventually, my heart is restored to warmth.

There is great power in the group. My community of eighty-five nuns carries me when my devotion is tepid. I see that same zeal among my Muslim friends. The stopping for prayer is the norm, allowing us to be God-conscious during the in-between times and to help God-consciousness become pervasive. What then happens is that we return to ritual prayer thankful for this felt presence of God. The combination of frequent gathering for prayer (as we do in the Divine Office) and the ceaseless prayer we do in our personal prayer (like saying the Jesus Prayer) allows us to keep the memory of God ever present. Doing this shifts consciousness from remembering that God is present to an abiding experience of God's Presence.

Many in the Christian world find the idea of ceaseless prayer strange. One time a classmate from my days at college stopped by the monastery and we were catching up after years of separation. "What do you do all day?" she asked me. How could I get anything done with all that prayer? Wasn't I tired of being a nun after forty years? I had no answer for her. This was the way I lived and the way all of us at the monastery lived. There was nothing else. It is in this lived reality—and the all-encompassing nature of it—whereby I feel kinship with Islam. We serve others—a natural outcome of all the praying.

3. Almsgiving *(zakat)*

The third pillar of Islam involves a serious redistribution of wealth. Since all is given by God, then nothing of what I own is mine, unless it is shared according to God's will. Muslims traditionally give 2.5 percent of their wealth to the poor, although this tithing sometimes has taken the form of a tax if the government is Muslim. Nevertheless, the intent remains the same: to give to the poor and to be a just and peace-filled society.

The principle of almsgiving stems from Muhammad's alarm at the sight of the poor during his early days as a traveling merchant. He witnessed the unjust burden of the masses and the opulence of the ruling families and decided that he and his followers would make sure that the poor had food, clothing and shelter. He saw that all creatures belonged to God and that Allah would repay each according to their good deeds on Earth and in heaven.

Muhammad had a keen sense of the hereafter, and the Qur'an describes heaven and the final days of Earth with rich imagery. At one of our dialogues, my Muslim friends and I talked about how we viewed the afterlife. The Muslims had clear portraits of the afterlife. We explained that as Catholics we had only the belief in the afterlife and that, while there is a rich artistic heritage depicting the afterlife, for Catholics, the Bible does not provide a portrait. The revelation in the Qur'an is that in this world the rich must give to the poor to guarantee a place in heaven with the angels and Allah. In practice, therefore, almsgiving is an insurance policy to be entitled to heaven. The gathering of alms also exemplifies to Muslims that they are an *umma*, a community.

Such generosity is based on two teachings. First, as we have seen, all goods are gifts of God and God has told us to share them. Secondly, these gifts are blessings and rewards from God and will be taken away if not used rightly. For Muslims, giving to the poor is not optional; it is the duty of bowing with one's goods. There are no exceptions—all are expected to give annually. In practice, this means that a Muslim who makes $40,000 gives about $1,000 off the net income.

The pillar of almsgiving seems eminently sensible, not only because a just society requires equity but because of the basic belief that earthly prosperity is the sacrament whereby God is mediated from heaven to Earth. Jews and Muslims establish a "this-worldly" goal of economic well-being as the proof of God's blessings. Muslims also have these riches continuing in a heavenly realm. Muslims believe that God wants His peoples to prosper and to live in rich abundance. Therefore, grace is not invisible, but instead visible through family, offspring, property, security and good order.

(As you can see, the pillars of Islam build an edifice. God is. God is One. There is no other God than Allah. Surrender. Obey, pray and create a just and peaceful society. Recite praise to Allah. Bow heads and bend knees five times a day. Give what has been given to those in need.)

In writing this, I know that there are Muslims, just as there are Christians, who are devout practitioners, and those who claim the name but dismiss the laws and customs. I suspect this might be true of all religious traditions. My feelings are that, as a large religion, Islam has room for all degrees of involvement. There is a strong belief in Islam that Allah will judge you, and there are many pictures of reward and punishment in the afterlife. Consequent to the idea of almsgiving and to the sense of judgment for one's life, Islam strongly hints at egalitarianism in daily life before there is eternal life. Giving to the poor is not a matter of mercy or charity on the devotee's behalf. It is a matter of justice.

For the Muslim, God does not plan for his creatures to be poor. A Muslim feels blessed for being alive and understands that he is created by God and so surrenders his life to God. As part of his surrender, *islam*, the Muslim provides for the poor and thus receives God's mercy and goodness through economic prosperity. This instills more gratitude as well as salvation in the hereafter, which stimulates still further surrender. In this way, Islam is firm, dynamic and actual—a universal pattern that God first set in motion at the Creation.

It is more than "a shame" to have the poor in our midst. For a Muslim, to mingle with the poor offends sensibilities and the Muslim has a mandate to do something about it. In fact, Muslims' eternal salvation depends on their response to justice. Where Christianity historically has been concerned about right doctrine (orthodoxy), Islam was from its inception primarily a way of right living (orthopraxy). In fact, not only could one argue that Islam is a response to pagan Arabia's failure to deal with poverty, but it is also a "reformation" of sixth-century Christian and Jewish indifference to the inequalities between rich and poor.

In Islam, the leadership is predominantly lay— although the distinction between lay and clergy has its own particular character since Shiite imams may sometimes behave in the same way as clergy. Nevertheless, it is fair to say that there is no Church or priestly class between the Muslim and God. There are mosques that are centers of worship, as well as of learning and study of the Qur'an, and these may raise up an imam as a leader. However, there is no formal ordination ceremony. The imams I have met qualified for their position by reciting the Qur'an and living the life with exactitude. As a religion, Islam has the minimum amount of infrastructure that requires overhead and maintenance. A mosque (the word itself literally means "a place to prostrate") is often stunningly beautiful architecturally and can be brilliantly ornate. However, all semblance of opulence is to be avoided and most staff workers are volunteers. The money collected usually goes to those in need through education loans, financial opportunities, or in the basics of food, medicine, clothing and shelter in the attendees' countries of origin, many of which have been devastated by war.

Mosques have regular training for children and provide places for marriage and funerals and the ongoing socialization of the Muslim way of life. In Plainfield, Indiana, the mosque has a full-time staff member who helps to arrange marriages and assist the next generation in perpetuating their Muslim heritage.

It has been a gradual revelation to me how closely interwoven in community and family are the lives of my Muslim friends. Catholicism in America has been through the turn of modernity and the secularism and separation of Church and State. First-generation Muslims have come to the United States from a variety of countries that have kept the sacredness of their faith with a worldview where there has been no separation of the religion of Islam from being a Muslim, an American, a doctor, a father, a husband, etc. In this regard, their lives mirror my own as a nun. When asked what our mission is, nuns respond that our monastic way of life is God's way for us and is a benefit for all humankind. I believe a Muslim would say that Islam is the whole of their way of life, with nothing outside of it. It deserves, and gets, total loyalty and commitment.

4. Ramadan

The fourth pillar of Islam is the fast that takes place during the holy month of Ramadan, the ninth month of the Muslim calendar. It lasts from the first sighting of the crescent moon until the next first sighting of the crescent moon, which ends the fasting with a meal of celebration. The emblem of the crescent moon is an identifying symbol for Islam. All Muslims all over the world during Ramadan are called on to fast for thirty days, unless they are sick or on a journey. The aim of abstaining from food during the day is to help Muslims identify with the poor, who cannot choose when, where and what to eat. In this way, fasting is similar in intention to almsgiving. Because the Muslim calendar has 354 or 355 days in it, Ramadan each year occurs ten days earlier than the previous year, although the length of time the fasting occurs is always thirty days. As David Noss puts it:

> [A]s soon as it becomes possible at dawn to distinguish a white thread from a black one, no food or drink may be taken until sun-down; then enough food or drink should be consumed to enable one to fast the next day without physical weakness.[3]

Several traditions have grown up regarding the meal that occurs after the sun has gone down. For some, the meal is a time of celebration and story telling. For others it is an ascetical practice of remembering the Prophet, his mission and all the hardships he endured in the name of God. The close of the month is usually celebrated in a great festival called Eid. Just as Easter is a time of joy at the end of Lent, so Eid is a time when the purification that fasting provides can be truly felt.

Fasting is a practice that appears in some manner through all the major religions, and it has major benefits. Voluntary fasting sets one apart from the mundane, gives them discipline and provides a physical dimension to beliefs that otherwise might simply be only an assent of words. Fasting necessitates resisting one's needs and desires and self-will by surrendering them to God's will.

In comparison with some practices of fasting in other world religions, Ramadan is a moderate fast. It only lasts one month and takes place only during the daylight hours. It requires no special foods and can be done by anyone anywhere. Like other fasts, it teaches discernment and creates a culture of restraint. The fast from food and drink takes place in the midst of the ordinary day, during which each Muslim prays five times a day and does his duty of work. During Ramadan, the Muslim is to refrain from sexual activity—a practice that, along with the training of thirty days of fasting with a like-minded group, exemplifies and influences other forms of restraint from self-indulgence. As suggested before, there is a direct link between fasting and almsgiving. The observant Muslim is called to surrender, again not in idealism, but in actuality and at an ordinary level whereby fasting is simply seen as what it

means to be a Muslim. In other words, these practices are
not, as Christians might imagine, the higher practices of a
saint. They are the expected minimum activity of ordinary
people.

5. Pilgrimage

The fifth pillar of Islam also bonds a community of
believers. It is the pilgrimage (*hajj*) to Mecca. This obliga-
tion does what all great pilgrimages do: it restarts the
conversion experience by returning the devotee to the point
of origin. A religion is not just a collectivity, but consists of
many clusters of individuals who must take on themselves
again the beliefs and practices of the founder of the religion
and the dictates of the religion's scriptures. To take a sacred
journey, along with other believers, is to personally accept
and immerse oneself in the culture of that religion and
make it your own.

The customs surrounding the Muslim pilgrimage are
instructive. All men, and all women accompanied by a
male, can go the *hajj* if they can afford it. In the ceremony,
all males, whether rich or poor, enter the precincts of
Mecca wearing the same kind of seamless white garments.
They practice the proper abstinence—no food or drink by
day, sexual continence, and no harm to living things. No
exceptions are made for class, race or nationality. The
ritual takes the form of a circumambulation of the Kaaba,
a sacred stone of great religious significance in pagan
Arabia that maintained its sacredness in Islam. Legend has

it that God gave the stone to Adam on his expulsion from paradise so that his sins could be forgiven.

The pilgrims start at the Kaaba and run three times fast and four times slowly around the building that houses the stone, stopping each time at the southeast corner to kiss the stone itself. If the crowd is too great, pilgrims can touch it with hand or stick or perhaps just look at it with eagerness and devotion. It is said that the stone used to be white in color, but turned black from absorbing the sins of all the devotees who have touched or kissed it. The next observance is the Lesser Pilgrimage, which consists of trotting, with shoulders shaking, seven times between Safa and Marwa, two low hills across the valley from each other. This ritual is in imitation of the frantic Hagar, the wife of Abraham, desperately seeking water for her baby, Ishmael, whose children are thought to be the ancestors of Muslims, just as Isaac, son of Abraham's wife Sarah, is said to be patriarch of the Jews.

On the eighth day of the *hajj*, the Greater Pilgrimage begins. The pilgrims, in a dense mass, move off toward the Arafat plain, nine miles to the east. They pass the night at Mina, a place halfway between Mecca and Arafat. The next day, all pilgrims arrive at the Arafat plain, where they engage in a prayer service conducted by an imam, listen to his sermon, and, of utmost importance, stand or move slowly about, absorbed in pious meditation. After sunset, they begin running en masse with enormous joy and commotion to Muzdalifah, which is a quarter of the distance back to Mecca, where they pass the night in the open. At sunrise, they continue to Mina, where each pilgrim casts seven pebbles at three places (in order to ward off demons) down the slope below the mountain road, crying out at each throw, "In the name of God! Allah is almighty!" Next there is a sacrificial offering of meat (to represent Abraham's sacrifice of the ram to God) and the meat is eaten by all.

The three days following are spent in eating, talking and merrymaking, in the strictest continence, and then as a final act of the pilgrimage all return to Mecca and make the circuit of the Kaaba once more.[4]

Lest a non-Muslim reader mistake the *hajj* as a solely ethnic practice and bracket the pilgrimage with the great pilgrimages to Jerusalem, Arunachala in India, Mount Kailas in Tibet or Lourdes in France, the Meccan pilgrimage is in a class of its own. There are over one billion Muslims in the world, and each male is required to make this pilgrimage once in his life. Devout women and young people are also admitted, which means that every year the numbers attending the *hajj* are huge—up to three million or more people at a time. Pilgrims must obtain a special visa stating that they are fit and observant Muslims. This pilgrimage of antiquity combines all the human and divine muscle to evoke and sustain conversion—travel from all nations of the world, the requirements of ritual purity, the wearing of special clothes, the walking over twenty miles, the night-sleep in open air, and the accommodations in tents pitched in the desert. It is an extraordinary effort of logistics and faith.

The recitation of the Qur'an in Arabic, the en masse salute, the fellowship of meals and hours of sharing and being a "people" surrendered to Allah make evident the literal meaning of religion as a "binding" to God. The *hajj* binds each Muslim to Allah and to every other Muslim. Uniquely, this binding is not restricted to the ordained or the vowed elite, or those who privilege a particular location for their form of devotion. To be a Muslim is to be beyond ethnic identity, and the pillar of this pilgrimage tells the story and incorporates each member, each generation and the people as a whole into the revelation given to the Prophet. The total experience is one of surrender, while the feeling generated in each person is of being a descendent of Abraham under God.

In Christianity, we often use the image of the desert to describe an experience on our spiritual journey. Christianity's earliest monastic tradition in the third century began in a desert that within four centuries was—as it is now—mostly in Muslim countries. The monks and nuns of those early Christian settlements were not in community as we live it today. They were hermits who went out to live the solitary life, motivated by the goal of praying without ceasing and seeking God with their whole attention. They met their inner demons that were the afflictions of food, sex, material possessions, anger, depression, acedia (spiritual soul fatigue), vainglory and pride. Grace prevailed.

These Desert Fathers and Mothers are the source of wisdom for the founder of the monastic order I live today as a Benedictine.

It is my belief that the desert of the pilgrimage expected of every Muslim is not unlike the protracted solitude in the desert, where the monastic faces his or her inner demons and surrenders his or her ego to God in utmost humility. Christ, too, before the advent of his ministry is driven by the Spirit into the desert to be tested (Mark 1:12). The desert clarifies the mind and purges the soul; it is real and symbolic. In the real geographic location one must stay focused to survive, one must get along with others to secure and maintain goods, one must move quickly, lightly and frequently to have enough basics for food, shelter, clothing and human interaction. One must be tough enough to travel long distances and defer one's needs to provide for those who are weak. One must enjoy the solitude and adapt to the climate's harshness.

The landscape of the symbolic desert forces one to cultivate an inner life, because there is no way to avoid feeling again and again all the thoughts, desires and passions that rise when the external world offers no distraction. The spiritual journey courses through the soul without the noise of crowds or the pressures of overwork. In such a situation a rawness or nakedness, a sense of being alone with the Alone, occurs. Hermits push themselves to the edge of being bound to the Earth in order to step out of time and into the temple of God's presence. Given the power of the desert, it makes sense that Muslims celebrate their origins in Arabia and take a pilgrimage through the desert in order to return to the core of their faith. The *hajj* thus actualizes the inner life of the spiritual journey in a communal experience. Most of us choose not to become hermits. However, it is reasonable to believe that once in our life we could make pilgrimage to Jerusalem or Mecca and in this way externalize our inner journey. By making the pilgrimage to Mecca one of its five pillars, Islam pulls together the meaning of the desert and the inner conversion necessary to surrender to one's depths during one's life. Once again, as we saw with fasting, it makes a serious religious practice—the inner spiritual journey—not simply a matter for saints or mystics or hermits. Islam makes the *hajj* a defining feature of being a Muslim.

In 1996, Monastic Interreligious Dialogue conducted a conference at Gethsemani Abbey, Kentucky (the home of Thomas Merton), where Buddhist and Christian monastics discussed their traditions in a spirit of tolerance and under-standing. One of the attendees was His Holiness the Dalai Lama, who suggested that pilgrimage would be a fitting follow-up to the hospitality and the dwelling together with one heart we had experienced. The hardships of pilgrimage, he noted, in themselves provide the purifica-tions necessary to remove obstacles to a clear mind and an open heart. The Dalai Lama said that pilgrimages situate dialogue on the human plane where there are no academic or doctrinal differences and no speculative talk about what someone else is doing somewhere else at another time. Pilgrimage is a human way that all humankind can be united in microcosm.

At the invitation of His Holiness the Dalai Lama we have been to Tibet and circumambulated the sacred sites with the Tibetan nomads. While the numbers were fewer than in Mecca, the zeal and absolute concentration in contemplative prayer shown by the pilgrims were life-changing and gave me something of an idea of what it must be like to be in Mecca. In the middle of these Buddhist nomads, at an altitude of 14,000 feet, I was swept into silence by the mantras, prayer wheels and chants anointing my soul. I can only imagine that a pilgrimage in the desert to Mecca would be the same transcendent experience.

The five pillars of Islam support a people dedicated to God. The *shahada* is the pole around which the essence of the Muslim faith—the transcendent experience of God—rotates. The other four pillars set in motion the surrender—prayer five times a day, almsgiving, fasting at Ramadan and the pilgrimage to Mecca. The formula is ingenious and holds a diverse people together while compelling individuals to perform this duty of right living and sharing with others.

Notes
1. Karen Armstrong, *Islam: A Short History* (New York: Modern Library, 2002), p. 8.

2. David S. Noss. *A History of the World's Religions* (Upper Saddle River: Simon & Schuster, 1994, Tenth Edition), p. 607.

3. Ibid., p. 546.

4. Ibid., pp. 547–8.

⊰ 4 ⊱

Insights into Islam

The Origin of Islam in the Desert

There have been a few themes that have emerged in the Muslim–Catholic dialogue that have given me insight into Islam. The first insight I have had is the shaping of Islam by its origins in the desert, which I talked briefly about at the end of the previous chapter. Muhammad was a merchant and not a nomad, but he spent a great deal of time alone in the desert and in caravans, crossing its great expanse. While Islam has appealed to the many cultures of the cities and towns in mountains and forests, I believe that its origins in the vastness of a desert and the scarcity of water, food and shelter created an archetypal psyche that had to be tough enough to "make do," to make sacrifices and to defer comfort. It encouraged thinking ahead, planning and using things in moderation, because what was at stake was not comfort and more ease but life or death.

In addition, there were the distances that needed to be traveled with few people around to help. Much effort was required to get from point to point transporting goods to barter with someone. Because of the threat of raids on one's caravan, there were strong incentives to bond together against common foes, to trust another's word and to count on a deal—all of which was offset against the vulnerability of being isolated because and for the sake of the harsh and unrelenting climate. The desert is fierce and only the strong can negotiate it. As with Tibetans in their mountainous terrain, one can assume that only the hardiest of Arab offspring, well adapted to live in such conditions, would survive. While the Islamic faith grew and absorbed non-desert-dwelling peoples such as Europeans, Africans, Asians and Americans, the origin of this religion has the strength of the desert. By thinking of Islam in this way—as a religion conceived in and toughened by the desert—we can see how it has endured from generation to generation and from country to country. It had built-in adaptation mechanisms and traveled fast and light—not weighed down by doctrinal baggage, political superstructure or symbolic overload: the perfect mode for traveling safely in the desert.

We might be so bold as to say that the desert does for the Muslims what the cross does for Christians—it unifies contradictions and saves. Its barrenness confronts one directly with God, without mediation or representation. The oases offer visions of heaven, and mirages demand that one be aware of illusion. The arc of the horizon forms a slow crescent moon, while the stars in the cloudless night sky above provide evidence of the miracle of creation and the necessary humility required to surrender to it. The starkness of the surrounding space opens up the opportunity for the transcendent God to fill it with all-merciful love.

In Indiana, we have four annual seasons of almost equal length. To me, the desert calls forth an abiding inner place beneath the flow of ordinary consciousness. It has its seasons, too, but its changes strike me as ancient and slow-moving, hidden and mysterious, but somehow *known* by us in our hearts. It helps me to understand Islam by thinking of it as the terrain of a desert, crossed by caravans that direct themselves solely toward God.

An Unmediated Symbol System

Islam provides a cohesive grid of inner strength using an unmediated symbol system. A social scientist might have crisper language to describe this insight, but as I sit at the table of dialogue with my Muslim friends I catch their three-dimensional faith: "There is no God but God; I surrender in awe, bending my knee and bowing my head; upon rising I live with others according to the Qur'an." Muslims, as people of the revelation of God spoken through the Qur'an, have a direct access to God through hearing those inspired words mediated by Muhammad.

One weekday morning a few years ago, Judith Cebula, religion reporter for the *Indianapolis Star*, interviewed Dr. Shahid Athar and his wife and myself for an article on women in Catholicism and Islam. Judith asked us why Islam was so attractive and was the fastest-growing reli-

gion in the world. I said that as a catechist I admired the
clarity of Islam; it was simply an easier religion to teach,
even though it was probably harder to live by. Dr. Athar
was surprised at my statement and asked me why I thought
Islam was so catechetically appealing. I told him that
Catholicism has at its heart the teaching of the Trinity—
Jesus, the Son of God, sent by the Father and leaving us
with the love of the Holy Spirit. In Islam, I noted, there is
One God, who provided a revelation mediated by the
Prophet Muhammad. There is no mediation of the Church
of Christ, but direct worship, duty and way of faith. While
Islam is complex, sophisticated and multi-layered in its
history, context, scholars and teachers, and in its vast array
of color and texture because of its size, many cultures and
artistic achievements, the faith system is still direct, imme-
diate, personal and specific.

Islam's particular focus has been mediation with God
through the possessions of this world. In Islam there do not
exist the "other worldly" sacraments such as the seven
sacraments of Catholics (baptism, confirmation, Eucharist,
penance, matrimony, last rites and ordination to the priesthood) or other signs and symbols of the blessing of God.
Like Jews, Muslims receive God's blessings through material prosperity as signs of approval and approbation. This
is not something unique to monotheism. Hindus also pray
to Lakshmi, the goddess of wealth and prosperity, and the
Tibetans to Vasudhara. The link with prosperity in Christianity is most often seen in Protestantism, but Catholicism

has certainly throughout its history often raised the acquisition of material wealth to a visible level of opulence. At one time, the Roman Church owned much of the territory of Europe. Monastics in my own tradition became landowners and aristocratic power brokers. All monotheistic religions believe at their core that if God is good, then goodness follows. In Christianity, however, the corrective to the acquisition of wealth is that it is better to renounce than to be weighted down with material goods, while in Islam, as we have seen, there is an egalitarianism that governs economic well-being for even the poorest of its members.

At one of the first Muslim–Catholic dialogues hosted at the Islamic Society of America, I asked if there was a video that would be good to view to learn more about Islam. I was given a video that said, "Islam is economic ascendancy under Allah." The sacrament for Muslims is an economic order where justice prevails, the poor are cared for and there is peace and well-being. There is no separation of Church and State. It is here, it seems to me, that the "this worldly" dimension needs to be grasped—that it is in *this* world that people surrender to God. Good will be rewarded both now and in eternity—a reward that comes directly from God and not through symbolic gestures or ritual sacraments. Earth is a sacrament and ordinary life is Islam's way of salvation. Blessings are material and visible signs of God's favor.[1]

When Muslims call Christians infidels, they are not complaining so much about our being unfaithful to doctrines about God as much as our failing to pursue the economic justice that is God's imperative for followers. With an unmediated symbol system (which means no Jesus Christ), there is naked presence between the transcendent God and the human's right living (righteousness). Consequent to my experience of dialogue with Islam, I have had to ask myself if I have misused my belief in Jesus, my Lord, in neglecting my part in helping others live. In one sense, there is no need for the separation of Church and State, as there is no Church to be distinct from. In Islam there is no middle term—only Allah and the People of God. There is also no "State," if we see the state as a person or group that can make decisions independently of God, because there is no secular, freestanding anything. All is under Allah. Allah blesses humans with the Earth and all its gifts. This understanding operates as the center of gravity for all political zones.

An extreme manifestation of this identity may be operating in Iran, which is ruled by clerics. Iran does not, as far as I am concerned, represent the natural or ultimate expression of the faithful Islamic state—given that there are faithful Muslims who live in all the democracies. Iran is more of a historical accident—rather like Christendom when it was governed under the Divine Right of Kings and when such religio-political entities as the Holy Roman Empire and the Papal States existed. The deeper point I now understand is that Islam's way of life is non-hierarchical and its wealth comes about as an expression of God's favor, in a way that is similar to the Jewish identification of "favor" through wealth. That can be in any nation or country; it is only the fundamentalist Jewish stream that insists on the historic property known as Israel with its center city, Jerusalem; and it is only fundamentalist Muslims that insist on Islamic "rule." A Christianity that follows Jesus' directives is neither political nor economic. Instead, it sees the reign of God as not of this world; we live here humanly engaged, neither needing to rule politically nor with prosperity or physical wealth sanctifying our lives.

Ascendancy View

What do I mean by "ascendancy" in the previous section? For Muslims, Islam is the one true faith in that it is the last revelation of the God of Abraham, Moses and Jesus. Through Muhammad, Muslims believe, the Islamic tradition of surrender is the fullest expression of belief, the direct way to God and the perfect relationship.

When participating in a meeting in Chicago, I visited a Bahai Temple in Wilmette, Illinois. The white, Persian architecture of a perfect temple to the heavens lifted my spirits and I delighted in its beauty. We came to the gathering space beneath the prayer hall to the welcoming center. There was a wall-sized histogram that plotted time from Adam, Abraham, Moses, Jesus, Muhammad and, in the largest, boldest, graphic, Bahaullah, the Persian founder of Bahai. In this case, all previous revelations were incorporated into the one great religious truth of the Kitab-I-Izan, "The Book of Certitude," of the Bahai faith. This graphic of ascendancy made my heart sink. I felt that Jesus the Christ was just a subset of this faith and not the Way, the Truth and the Light. If a Muslim had entered that welcome center, she or he would have had the same sinking feeling. The Prophet Muhammad was just one more prophet in the line of other distinguished prophets, who were all superseded and subsumed under the wings of the final prophet, Bahaullah of the Bahai. Since then, I have been in many dialogues that eventually come to this same impasse—each religion thinks of itself as the final and complete message of salvation. Father Bruno Barnhart, a monk at the Monastery of New Camaldoli in Big Sur, California, says that each religion fills out the entire landscape. It is natural to see history from our own point of view. We are not God.

Bernard Lewis picks a middle way between triumphalism and relativism when he says that human beings may use different religions to speak to God, as they use different languages to speak to one another, but that God understands them all.[2] From a dialogue point of view, I find it is helpful to speak my own experience and listen to my dialogue partner without judgment. The content is persons, not God. God can take care of Himself! Though revelation is certain, dogmas change with understanding and growth.

In a little book such as this, there is no place for an extended analysis of the sense of ascendancy that devotees of many faiths feel of their own faith. All adherents have an identity forged through their particular faith, which, at some level, makes it necessary for them to relate to another faith in a particular way. This is perhaps a function of human nature, a way to feel wholehearted in one's commitment. Feeling that sense of ascendancy creates solidarity, a sense of belonging and yet of being apart from others. Unfortunately, throughout human history, this feeling of ascendancy has had a negative side—which is to see the non-member of one's religion as someone who does not "belong" and is on a road to perdition unless he or she is saved. All religions, therefore, to some degree have a natural tendency to share their message and integrate it into society—what we Christians mean by "evangelize." Such an attitude, however, can leave no oxygen for others who have different beliefs to breathe.

Because of its sense of ascendancy, Islam has, like Christianity, undergone crisis after crisis. What makes Islam particularly vulnerable to the negative dimensions of a belief in ascendancy is the belief in God without division as well as the idea that it is in this lifetime that we will be blessed, as opposed to dwelling on the spiritual benefits of the life beyond. Therefore, ascendancy that is both economic, political and theological is on a collision course with other faiths and cultures. What all religious practitioners need to understand—especially religions that emphasize that their way of practice is "the Way, the Truth and the Life"—is that, as I say earlier, religion is not God. God is more than any religion. Religion is a human system for the human effort at relating to God. Consequently, it cannot be perfect and unique. In fact, some religious writers distinguish their faith tradition (be it Christianity, Buddhism, Islam or whatever) from religion as a human institution. The truth that Islamic ascendancy asserts is that God is and God is One. Other considerations need not detract from the pure form of God-consciousness.

Muslims believe God revealed to Muhammad a way to reconnect with our Creator through the path of surrender. That sense of surrender in and of itself offers a sense of ascendancy that in its totality is profound and profoundly meaningful. However, such a sense cannot be used as a template for "others." Extremists within Islam take the economic and theological sense of ascendancy as a literal truth that they wish to apply to all members and non-members of their faith. Moderate Muslims, particularly here in the United States, see their Islam as a personal practice that supports their work for self-determination. They experience the complexity of relating to a secular culture and maintaining their faith.

I should emphasize here that in none of our Muslim–Catholic dialogue sessions has there been anything but respect for the distinctions and differences between Islam and Catholicism expressed by either myself or my dialogists. We all feel energy and delight in getting to know and appreciating each other as the "other." What the United States offers my Muslim friends, many of whom are first-generation immigrants, as well as those who were born here seems to be the possibility of healthy pluralism. Living side by side with people of different cultural and religious backgrounds and working together with them on common "goods" for families, neighborhoods, country and the world is one of America's great gifts. Islam, as a global religion, has always had to negotiate with other religions, and in America it is negotiating its place in a democratic culture. The events of September 11, 2001 and other so-called Islamic terrorist activity before and since come out of a brand of Islam that is deeply alien to the vast majority of Muslims, just as the kind of evangelical Christianity that argues that one will go to Hell unless one is born again and that all non-Christians will go to hell for all eternity is deeply embarrassing to the vast majority of Christians. Unfortunately, fundamentalism manifests itself in all our religions, and it is always a source of conflict. I agree with Dr. Athar when he says that a religion cannot be judged by the behavior or wrong actions of those who claim to be born in that faith but who practice the opposite of what the faith teaches. In the next chapter I attempt to address the three questions most often asked of me by non-Muslims reacting to Islam in the world today.

Notes

1. *Islam: The Story of Islam. A History of the World's Most Misunderstood Faith.* MPI. Home Video, 1990.

2. Bernard Lewis. "I'm Right, You're Wrong, Go to Hell." *Atlantic Monthly,* Vol. 291 No. 4 May 2003, p. 39.

ᵈᵊ 5 ᵊᵈ

Three Questions

Over the seven years of dialogue my Muslim friends and I have had many technical conversations about the Bible and the Qur'an, the Prophet and Jesus Christ, the expectations of the afterlife, the moral codes and so forth. However, three themes have emerged, mostly from the Catholic side, that have begged for clarification: fundamentalism, women's rights and democratic principles.

1. Does Islam foster violent fundamentalism?

When people in the West talk about "Islamic fundamentalism," they are generally thinking of the very strict versions of Islam that seem to them to encourage martyrdom and foster highly repressive laws, especially for women. They are thinking of the kind of the Wahhabi-oriented Islam of Osama bin Laden and women covered from head to toe in clothing that makes it difficult for them to see or move around. They are thinking of the woman who was accused of having a child out of wedlock and was sentenced to death by stoning by an Islamic court in northern Nigeria, using a strict interpretation of *sharia* law.

They are thinking of the girls who are not allowed to go to school in Afghanistan or the women who are not allowed to drive in Saudi Arabia. Unfortunately, Christians themselves could detail story after story of the misguided zeal of fundamentalist and reactionary behaviors—from bombing abortion clinics to withholding medicine from a dying child, from expelling a pregnant adolescent girl from secondary school to Christian polygamy in Utah.

Muslims and Christians alike are appalled by the Christian leaders that liken Islam to Satanism.[1] Such hatred of another seems to be more than simple ignorance. Likewise, the Jungian theory that all of us have a "shadow" side that acts out unless integrated into the personality, or the stories about demons in our own scriptures, are inadequate as explanations of the disproportionate damage done to the innocent by these cruel and unfeeling actions. The Desert Fathers, speaking from experience, declare that those who judge others actually nourish the seeds of that same manifestation of evil in themselves, and that the more they judge others, the more vulnerable they are to the same sin that the accusers accuse the "other" of committing. The speck in the other's eye really is the beam in their own.

In a dialogue on purity of heart at New Camaldoli Monastery in Big Sur, California, Father William Skudlarek of St. John's Abbey wrote a paper on *zazen* entitled "A Path from Judgment to Love." He took the meaning of the Desert Fathers even deeper: Jesus' words on not judging, he said, were not about the subject or object of one's judgment. If a practitioner judges, that practitioner is not a practitioner. We must love with the same love that God loves us in Jesus.[2]

I will never forget one particular session of Muslim–Catholic dialogue just days after September 11, 2001, when several of us gathered together to discuss what had happened. We were from India, Pakistan, Iran and Palestine, now living in St. Louis, Detroit, Toledo, Louisville, Indianapolis, Chicago and Washington, DC. The Muslims recounted story after story of anti-Muslim retaliation, balanced by warm letters they had received from Catholic school children, as well as visits and donations. When the Muslims' windows had been smashed, Christians had come over to help mend them, and in so doing had mended more than windows. I could feel the dense sadness and protracted silence that lay within our common heart and between our shared tears. American dreams had been shattered. We went on with our work collaborating on a paper on God's Word and the word of God.

Fundamentalist adherents seem to be clustered in small or large groups who feel rejected by their own membership. As believers they feel strongly, indeed passionately, about their faith and are zealous in practicing the required duties. They tend to accept the revelation, the law or the customs associated with their faith literally, with no interpretation other than their own. Their aim is to move from making themselves and their associates more faithful to their faith's message of peace and worship to converting unbelievers. When their efforts are rebuffed, the zeal coalesces into rage, and rage begets violence as the fundamentalist seeks to get the "other" to conform. To the extent that the beliefs and practices of Islam are clear and there is a strong tendency toward both material and theological ascendancy, fundamentalism as a fanatical force can have room to develop.

In one of our Buddhist–Catholic dialogues a monk called me to say that he was not able to come because an evangelical Protestant missionary group was proselytizing in his village in Burma, and his family had asked him to come home to stop the persecution of Buddhists by Christians in their town. Christians were burning Buddhist homes and businesses. There are far too many examples in history of violence caused by religious zeal. Catholics still blush with shame at the Crusades, the horrors of the Inquisition, and our tacit approval of Jewish persecution in Europe, which culminated in the Holocaust. In 1992, Monastic Interreligious Dialogue forged a declaration, signed by many religious leaders, that religion can no longer be used as a reason for war. The Church, especially through the many visits of our current pope, John Paul II, has been indefatigable on behalf of reconciliation.

One of the monks who was deeply involved in Catholic–Muslim relations was the Superior at the Trappist Monastery of Atlas in Algiers, where, in June 1996, five Christian monks were abducted and beheaded. Abbot

Armand Veilleux accompanied the Trappist Superior General to Algiers from Rome to identify the bodies of the slain monks. When I asked the abbot if he thought Islam was a religion that had core beliefs that led to violence, he told me the following:

> What did I learn about Islam in the contacts I had with Muslims? I think I would stress the fact that the "normal" Muslim is a deeply religious and usually peace-loving person. Fanaticism and terrorism are not representative of the Muslim world and certainly not of Islam. They are representative of a small percentage of Muslims. And we should add these Muslims are pushed towards fanaticism by the aggression and the unfairness of the Western countries. When people are deprived of their rights, are humiliated and left without any hope for a better future, recourse to violence is almost unavoidable.[3]

Abbot Armand's response forced me to think about my own faith. Did Catholicism, at its core, foster violence in the name of its faith? I sincerely believe that the answer is no. Both Catholicism and Islam have, at their core, teachings concerning peace and harmony among all nations. Both Islam and Catholicism have to travel the journey of faith toward their own way, truth and life, and not fight to destroy the "other" ways of reaching that goal.

I have learned in the Muslim–Catholic dialogue that
Islam has a rich tradition of right action and training in
ethics not unlike Buddhism. Dr. Athar, a physician, has a
strong teaching on "lying" as a disease of the spiritual heart:

> Lying is against human nature, against physiology,
> and, like a disease, has its own signs and symptoms.
> The act of lying produces inner conflicts between
> various control centers of the brain. The moment
> one begins to lie, the body sends out contradictory
> signals to cause facial muscle twitching, expansion
> and contraction of pupils, perspiration, flushing of
> cheeks, increased eye blinking, tremor of hand and
> rapid heart rate. These constitute the basis of lie
> detector instruments. In addition you will notice
> the liar is unconsciously doing some movements
> like covering his mouth, nose touching, eye
> rubbing, scratching the side of the neck, cupping
> his ear, etc. One of the clearest signs is that the liar
> keeps his palms closed and eyes pointed to another
> direction rather than facing the person eye to eye
> when he is lying. A liar is aware of his body signals,
> therefore he finds lying easier when no one can see
> him, i.e., on the phone or in writing.

Dr. Athar goes on to discuss motives for lying—if it is
ever justified—and the value of truth: "Truthfulness is a
command of God, part of faith, and an essential quality for

all prophets and is mentioned in one hundred places in the Qur'an."[4]

Violence is like lying. It is my understanding of Islam that not only are Muslims offended by the "bad zeal" of fundamentalist groups, but they are striving for ethical personal practices with good zeal that would make all of us saints if we followed the directives of the Qur'an.

2. What about women's equality?

Another question that constantly occurs in Muslim–Catholic dialogue is whether Islam is inherently opposed to women's equality with men or we can attribute the apparent oppression of women to a cultural time-lag. This question is one that we Catholic women also pose to our Church leaders—usually around the sticking point of ordination to the priesthood. In my experience, many women religious and lay believers question the theological reason why women cannot be ordained in the Roman rite (that Jesus did not appoint any women among his twelve disciples). They feel that the reason is more cultural than theological. I personally do not feel called to be ordained to the priesthood, but I respect deeply those men and women who do, and I feel that Catholics would be served well and well served by women priests, as well as they are now being served by married priests who have converted to Catholicism. This opinion, I should add, is not confined to my fellow women religious. Most of my male priest friends and associates state the same preference.

It is my belief that in time the Vatican will soften on this issue and that more married men and women will be ordained—the aging of the celibate male priesthood and the devotion and energy of women will make it both a necessity and a great source of joy and vigor for the Church. The issue of gender as a requirement for ordination is for me one governed by history, and, like most historical issues, this one will be resolved over time. The obstacles will fall away and the reasons that were used in support of disciplinary action or doctrinal rigidity will fall away as well.

I suspect that the issues that some women have regarding their role in Islam could stem from the same cultural time sequence. In my dialogue sessions with Muslims, men and women come together. From informal talks I have had with the women, I have learned how each country of their countries of origin has a range of observances that govern the role, dress and functions of women. There are liberal and conservative groups within each country, although women are emerging as autonomous and powerful presences in all countries around the world. There are Muslim organizations working on behalf of women and supporting their struggles around the world. Just as there is no spokesperson representing all Catholic women, so there is no unified voice for Muslim women.

In all societies and countries throughout the world, women's roles are changing. Less and less is marriage viewed as a tidy partnership that demands a wife's unquestioning submission to her husband or a husband's absolute domination of his wife. Children raised today do not automatically have the same values of their parents. This transition for many societies, both Muslim and non-Muslim, can be difficult.

Is it harder, however, for Muslim women to change? Is there anything intrinsic to Islam that curtails women's freedom?

To a degree, the answer has to be no. Women's lives throughout history and under many different faith practices have been extraordinarily difficult. Even today, women and children make up the majority of the world's poor, and forced marriages and lack of access to health care for bringing children into this world are still widespread throughout the world. We need to remember that Christianity was, quite literally, brought into the world through a pregnant, unwed teenager, Mary—a plight mirrored in countless young women's lives around the globe.

That said—and this is only the opinion of a nun, and an opinion offered humbly—I feel that Islam grew up in a culture of toughness that will only soften its edges as it applies its own values of egalitarian principles to gender roles.[5]

The fact of the desert, the direct access to God without mediation of symbols, and a rigorous prayer life both in public and in the home that is male-dominated gives me the impression that women will need special affirmation to be equal partners. Islam spread through conquest and consolidation, with an emphasis on education, feats of arms and an assembly at prayer that, even today, does not allow women in the main area of the mosque. Nevertheless, Islam places a special emphasis on the protection and care of, as well as respect for, women. Indeed, Muhammad took the lead in insisting on a woman's right to divorce, the possession of property and the learning of the Qur'an (admittedly at home and under the guidance of men).[6] Unlike in Christianity, there are no images of God, male or female, so God is not automatically viewed as an old man with a white beard. That said, it is the man rather than the woman who is assumed to be the leader of the family under God.

Change, when it happens, can happen quickly. When I grew up in the 1950s my father and his brothers went into business together. My father's four sisters were excluded from the partnership. My siblings went to Catholic schools from first grade through college and my mother thought of no work other than being a homemaker. My father led the rosary, the meal prayers, drove the car and passed his business on to his oldest son. Nowadays, this is changing, and the gender roles are blurring. It is not surprising that immigrant families from Asia and the Middle East moving to America or Europe experience culture shock.

In monastic orders, things are also changing. When I entered the convent in September 1961, I was given the black long skirt and short veil of a postulant. By May 1962, I was invested with the traditional black wool serge habit and a veil that extended to the back of my knees. I had a coif that covered my face, a dress dating back to the ninth century that went to the floor, and sleeves that amply covered all but my hands. I wore this or its modifications for almost fourteen years. I think that it is highly problematic for men to dictate a woman's dress. While I felt happy wearing an identifying garment that expressed my vowed life, I also felt that the black habit was a barrier between me and the students I taught.

Most women in the "developed" world are appalled by what they see as the "control" of women in the "undeveloped" world; although it would be worth examining our own "developed" assumptions about the "freedom" given to women through fashion, advertising and pornography. What "Western" women do not take account of, however, is that there are some women who *choose* to wear the *hijab* for symbolic and safety reasons. Throughout the centuries and in all countries, clothes (except, it often seems, in ritual) change and adapt to the times. I do not wear the veil today because to me it says more about division and disdain for the human community than it does about reverence for the awesome vocation to religious vows.

Women are represented in Islam in other ways. In her work on women and Islam, scholar Annemarie Schimmel has emphasized the feminine dimension of Islam[7] through the Sufi poems of the female mystic Rabia, the Turkish poet Rumi and others.

I feel I have an affinity with Sufi devotees. Their practices have heightened God-consciousness and have inspired
some of the greatest religious poetry and music ever
written. When I am with Sufis and participate in the prayer
to our same God, I feel their intensity. Some of that intensity's exuberance seems more like the Christian charismatic
movements than the low-key, everyday chant of the
monastic choir. Nevertheless, the sober phases of Sufism
seem like a great "fit" with my own love for Our Lord,
Jesus Christ—through our daily inner conversations.
Sufism is a way of love.[8]

Sufism shares with monasticism a course that runs
counter to fundamentalist approaches to religion. This is
because the mystical experience repeatedly transcends
doctrinal and institutional policies. Both Sufism and
monasticism are happily marginal to mainstream society.
Some prefer to use the word "liminal"—as in "crossing the
threshold"—to describe the movement to a contemplative
way of life both inside and out revealed in these practices.
Whatever the phrase, the way of love goes to the heart of
spiritual practice.

I have been warmed by the mysticism of the heart
present in Sufism. As I prepared for the dialogue on Purity
of Heart held in 2000, a dialogue between a Sufi and
Thomas Merton, the great Trappist scholar and instigator
of interreligious dialogue, caught my attention—as a
woman and practitioner with a deep sense of the feminine.[9]
In his reflections on the contemplative life, Merton talks of

le point vierge, a place of absolute purity—a spotless spot, as it were—untouchable by sin. Although the metaphor of the virginal point naturally has a sexual component, the concept transcends sexuality or gender. While *le point vierge* is indeed a place of conception and inception, where the mystery of life meets the miracle of birth, *le point vierge* is, more completely, the central point where, in apparent despair, one meets God and is found completely in His mercy.[10] It is a profoundly *pure* meeting-point—essential, sinless, forever new. I believe that Sufism offers a similar point of purity in its heart-centered practice. The word "devotion" is sometimes denigrated as denoting a superficial or irrational form of worship, but Sufi devotion, I feel, makes a deep avowal to life with God—an avowal as sacred as a marriage between partners.

Sufis practice what is known as the "science of hearts." Sufism began its development of Islamic mysticism by identifying anomalies in the spiritual life of the believer who prays and who must be simple and naked. This analysis served to designate the errors of judgment, the mental pretenses and the hypocrisies of the spiritual life—thus tearing away the barriers between the devotee and God. In this instance, the "heart" represents the incessant oscillation of the human will that beats under the impulse of various passions, an impulse that must be stabilized by the Essential Desire, the One God. Introspection must guide us to tear through the concentric "veils" that ensheath the heart and hide from us the immaculate or virginal point (*le point vierge*) or, in Sufi terms, the secret (*sirr*), wherein God manifests Himself.[11]

I, myself, have also found a sense of the feminine in Islam's wonderful teachings on angels. In Islam, the devout feel the presence of angels everywhere!

For the most part, Islam's cultural patterns and religious values are tightly woven and women are as bound to their position in their cultures as men are. It is often easier to stay in a constrained situation that you know than to seek the freedom of true equality—for both men and women—in a way that is unfamiliar. This is not something unique to Islam or the cultures in which Islam has flourished. I am an American woman and, in spite of the great strides made by women over the last century, I can attest that I am still not an equal partner in many aspects of my life with a man. As I watch my nieces grow into women I see this changing in a natural, mutually positive way.

None of this cultural conditioning and time-boundedness should be surprising. Religion binds things together in negative as well as positive ways. It gathers the values of the society in which it is practiced and stores the archives of the history of the religion in that society and tries to make both relevant for the next generation. The challenge is to make the classic memories and trusted practices of generations ago accessible to the contemporary members of society without forcing them to live in the past. Where all of us need to be vigilant is in not allowing oppression and repression to occur in our respective religious traditions through those in power falling back on expressions such as "God said so," simply to maintain their cultural and political dominance. God is beyond such petty political maneuvering.

It is a contention of the women's movement in the United States that the oppression of women is the oppression of men, too. It is time-consuming and enervating to try to control everything about your world, including the practice of others who simply share similar enthusiasms and a love of God. We women religious believe that men should be relieved of some of the burden of their responsibility and share in the joy, honor and responsibility of being worshippers and celebrants of God. None of us should use our religion to justify the oppression of women—whether Muslim or Christian, Buddhist or Jew. Additionally, from a spiritual point of view, there is a benefit in transcending gender-consciousness to lead to God-consciousness. That transcendence exerts compassion for all, regardless of gender, race, nationality, rank or geographic boundaries. After all, awareness of gender can be manipulated through simply transferring domination from one gender to another or retaliating angrily. Sometimes we all need to practice humility and charity rather than stridency or making demands. Civility and a sincere wish for the other's benefit are both the content and process of dialogue at its best.

3. Can Islam be democratic?

Finally, we need to ask about whether Islam can adapt to democratic principles. The simplest answer is, yes, it can. Turkey is almost wholly Islamic and it is a democracy, although there have been a number of coups over the years by a military fiercely dedicated to making sure that the state is secular, and there remains a troubling abuse of human rights, especially against the Kurdish minority. Indonesia, a majority Muslim country, after years of brutal dictatorship, is now a democracy, although anti-Christian and anti-Chinese riots are a disturbing reality and the country is far from stable. The world's largest democracy, India, has a population of over 120 million Muslims. Muslims have enjoyed representation in Parliament since independence, although the power of the Hindu nationalist Bharatiya Janata Party or BJP is at the time of this writing cause for concern, and the sporadic fighting between Hindus and Muslims in parts of India and the tension between India and Pakistan threaten to tear the country apart. It is worth noting that democratic Muslim countries have seen several women prime ministers: Benazir Bhutto in then-democratic Pakistan, Megawati Sukarnoputri in today's Indonesia, Begum Khaleda Zia in Bangladesh in 1991 and Sheikh Hasina Wajed in 1996, and Tansu Çiller in Turkey in the mid-1990s.

The issue, therefore, is not whether Islam can adapt to democracy, but whether Islam can live comfortably in a pluralistic and secular society that uniformly respects human rights and the rule of law but does not privilege any religion in its law or media. Again, I see no reason why this cannot happen—it is happening throughout Europe and in the United States, where many Muslims have thrived. Muslims have taken on leadership positions in many communities throughout the world, winning election to city councils, regional boards, and even in parliaments throughout Europe. Their educational discipline and business acumen have given Muslims opportunities to lift a whole population: the renaissance of the town of Leicester in the British Midlands, for instance, has often been credited to the influx of many South Asian Muslims who renovated houses and brought back businesses long lost to urban blight.

The challenge Muslims face is the challenge that all religious practitioners in Western democracies have had to face—to recognize the right of "others" to practice their faith and to acknowledge that other person's practice of faith is as true to him or her as their own is to them. No religion *can* be the dominant way to God. A theocracy cannot sustain pluralistic values: it is simply a contradiction in terms. We Catholics have had difficulty finding language that says how we feel: we love Jesus Christ and are confident in our salvation though Christ. All the various ways of sharing this belief risk being a judgment of another's path. I have come to the realization that Islam *is*, it just *is*, and we Catholics can wholeheartedly appreciate it as a means to God. From the original points of our initiations into faith we can live side by side, living fully as Christians and Muslims in a family larger than each of us and all of us put together.

Ironically, it has been dialogue with Buddhists that has helped me with a measured language about God. One of St. Benedict's teachers, John Cassian of the fourth century, spoke of renunciation of our "thought" of God because any "thought" is not God, but a human action. Therefore, at the deepest level of my heart I have to renounce my "thought" of God, because that thought is not God. In other words, I must learn to let God be God. It is this profound mystery and deep reverence that I place before my Muslim friends as they speak wholeheartedly to their One God beyond all names. Can we live on the same planet with the same earth under our feet and the name of the same God of the Heavens as we see it? I certainly think we can.

At a meeting held at Gethsemani Abbey in Kentucky in April 2002, an event known as "Gethsemani Encounter II," Fordham University professor of theology Father Leo Lefebure challenged the Christians among us to get beyond a narrow theism that makes "God" look bad.[12] God, he told us, cannot be a function of our ego, nor can it be a wedge for divisions and oppression. As the great medieval German mystic Meister Eckhart would have it, God is really "not-God" because we, God's creatures, are not the proper ones to "define" Him—if we were, we would be God! To me, in the face of this mystery, silence and adoration, or the bow of the Muslim five times a day, is the proper gesture.

In helping Islam adapt itself to the postmodern, postindustrial, globalized world of pluralistic culture and individualized faith, it is important that the West take very seriously the effect of its own secularism on people of faith, wherever they may come from. Since September 11, 2001, and the attack on the Pentagon and the World Trade Center, the United States and other majority non-Muslim nations have had to try to understand Islam from the ground up. Our ignorance has been revealed to us and our intolerance has not been attractive. Our common goal as Muslims and Christians has to be the instillation of the best of democracy in all our hearts. We must begin to dialogue about what is just or unjust aggression and out of what sense of humiliation come the horrors of terrorism. (In Louay M. Safi's *Peace and the Limits of War: Transcending Classical Conception of Jihad* we have a clear teaching on the Islamic notion of war and peace written after September 11).[13] I have appreciated the cautionary words of Dr. Hassan Hathout, Director of Outreach at the Islamic Center of Southern California. Just like communism, says Dr. Hathout, capitalism is inherently materialistic. Democracy can just be another oppressive ideology that substitutes individualism and risks the common good. Western culture's biggest threat to humankind is materialism and self-seeking.[14]

Catholicism and Islam share a similar vision of themselves as religions of peace. We have both learned in our long and uncomfortable history of confrontation and mutual disregard that violence begets violence. We both know that in our objectification and vilification of the "other" we take on the worst aspects of the one we hate. Americans cannot insist on democracy that has an agenda of forwarding only their own economic interests. Islamic countries must acknowledge individual rights and practice tolerance for, as well as safeguard in law, the right to free speech and assembly. All societies must condemn *all* acts of terrorism. Neither Islamic nor Christian political leaders should establish an agenda in which the one is defined as "good" and the "other" is defined as "evil." This is for God to decide. God respects the free will of choice based on the individual's conscience. To put it another way, oppression is oppression whatever part of the religious or political spectrum it comes from.

Is there an answer to the tyranny of theocratic, economic and ideological ascendancy? I believe that there is—and the answer is dialogue. Catholics are just now beginning to learn the lesson that we can affirm the truth, beauty and goodness of faith wherever we meet it. Through dialogue, we are beginning to understand the great wisdom traditions of the world and are finding ourselves surprised and delighted by similarities as well as challenged and deepened by differences. We are acknowledging that while we may never understand the full *richness* of the other's religion, we all have a deep commitment to the *poor*, who can teach us how to love and be loving as a way of life.

Notes

1. In "Religion and Satanism," dated April 10, 2002. The Calcedon Foundation. <http://www.chalcedon.edu/report/2002apr/blumenfeld. shtml>, viewed March 23, 2003.
2. William Skudlarek, OSB, "Zazen: From Judgment to Love," in *Purity of Heart and Contemplation*, edited by Bruno Barnhart and Joseph Wong (New York: Continuum, 2001), p. 149.
3. Armand Veilleux, personal correspondence, Sunday March 9, 2003.
4. Shahid Athar, *Reflections of an American Muslim*. (Chicago: Kazi Publications, 1994), p. 202.
5. "Status of Woman in Islam," Islamic Circle of North America. This little flyer consolidates current teachings on the issue. It is available from ICNA, 166-26 89th Avenue, Jamaica, NY 11432, Tel.: 718-658-1198 or 1-800-662-ISLAM. The pamphlet shows the Prophet's openness to women for his times and carries forward the most wholesome directions of this most sensitive human issue.
6. Karen Armstrong. *Muhammad: A Biography of the Prophet* (San Francisco: HarperSanFrancisco, 2001), p. 198.
7. Annemarie Schimmel. *My Soul is a Woman: The Feminine in Islam* (New York: Continuum, 1994).
8. Carl W. Ernst, PhD. *Sufism: An Essential Introduction to the Philosophy and Practice of the Mystical Tradition of Islam.* (Boston/London: Shambhala, 1997).
9. Barnhart and Wong. *Purity of Heart and Contemplation*.
10. Rob Baker and Gray Henry, editors. *Merton and Sufism: The Untold Story* (Louisville KY: Fons Vitae, 1999), p. 64.
11. Ibid. p. 66.
12. See the Gethsemani Encounter II at http://www.monasticdialog.com.
13. 2002. Available from the International Institute of Islamic Thought, PO Box 669, Herndon, VA 20172-0669.

14. Hassan Hathout. *Reading the Muslim Mind* (Burr Ridge, IL: American Trust Publications, 1995), p. 90.

≠ 6 ≈

Conclusion

In this little book I have tried to present a clear picture of Islam for Western minds with open hearts. I appreciate the five pillars as ingenious practices that make Islam a great religion, and I can see why so many accept their good example and become Muslim. I have outlined four traits of Islam not as hard-and-fast truths but as insights that have helped me understand where a Muslim dialogue partner is coming from.

My journey of understanding is just beginning. I intend to learn more about the Holy Prophet Muhammad and the sacred revelation of the Qur'an. I hope to study further the origins of Islam, founded by Muhammad from his desert home. I have argued that Islam has a cohesiveness that is unmediated by sign and symbol other than the five pillars and the way of life taught in the Qur'an, and that Christians would better understand Islam if we took note of the Muslim belief in sacramentality embedded in earthly prosperity. I have also suggested that Christians need to be fully aware of the Muslim belief in the sacredness of the Qur'an and Muhammad as the final and last prophet. And, lastly,

I have looked at three controversial questions regarding Islam—fundamentalism, women's equality and the democratic potential of Islamic states. I know that I have simply introduced and certainly not resolved these issues, but I wanted to share how these issues are spoken of with courage and candor at the table of the scholars, imams, physicians, nuns, priests, bishops, theologians and scholars with whom I have been in dialogue. That these questions can be raised at all is because my Muslim friends are not afraid to speak to these issues with wit and wisdom. When we *know* and *respect* each other, this kind of face-to-face dialogue becomes human and natural and beautiful.

Who, therefore, is a Muslim? A Muslim is someone who believes that there is no God but Allah, and that Muhammad is Allah's messenger—it is that simple and that direct. The Muslim sees the imprint of God in everything and everyone because we are all God's creatures. Through the pillars of the practice of his or her faith, the Muslim expresses his or her belief in God and in so doing joins him- or herself to all other believers who submit to Allah.

A Muslim is bound to give money to the poor, but he does not renounce wealth. He fasts for one month and does not eat pork, but eats normally the other eleven months of the year. A Muslim is obligated to make a pilgrimage to Mecca at least once in his lifetime; but if he is unable to go through sickness or poverty he can perform charitable acts at home. A Muslim bows five times a day to Allah and recites the prayers from his heart day in and day out, whether alone or with other Muslims, from morning until bedtime, punctuating the day with prayer inspired by faith. A Muslim knows the Qur'an, the customs and laws, and follows them wholeheartedly in this world with eager expectations of eternal life.

Islam in this regard is not a set of precepts to aspire to or a set of symbols of perfection. Islam is a lived and earthly existence governed by a direct connection to God in a life of surrender. Islam is a revealed pattern of being human that exists to create order from chaos—which is perhaps why Islamic culture has so often excelled in mathematics and science, architecture and calligraphy.

Some may feel that it is strange that I should argue, as I have in this book, that Islam, a most earthly religion, is nevertheless a fully formed vehicle toward God-consciousness. Islam is, indeed, earthly. The five pillars combined knot each human forehead to the earth five times a day before God's mercy, gathering the people of God together every day and then, in a ritual of origin, once in a lifetime at Mecca. By calling the faithful to Mecca, Islam allows each Muslim to be embodied historically in a place and demands that each Muslim share his financial and physical blessings with the poor. The Muslim recites his creed from what I like to call a memorized heart—where the inspiration and expiration of God through the repetition of the fact of the one God and Muhammad, His messenger, operates like the systole and diastole of the heart. Likewise, through the Halal laws and the period of Ramadan, the

Muslim refrains from food that is empty of God. It is, indeed, intensely physical. Yet it is this very physicality, this *earthiness*, that points the way to transcendence and God-consciousness.

As we have seen in this book, and throughout history, Islam has the power to initiate and sustain God-consciousness in persons and entire civilizations. And now Islam is with us in the United States and throughout the West—a jewel in our midst. It is a religion that brings each generation to a God-consciousness that fosters all that is human. Whether we are lay or religious, Christian or Muslim, we cannot afford to delegate this dialogue to specialists, academics, politicians and military generals. We must bow our heads and bend our knees and, upon rising, extend our hands. We are friends.

AFTERWORD

Shahid Athar, MD, FACE, FACP

It is a strange world indeed. A Catholic nun has asked her Muslim friend to write this postscript about her monograph on Islam. As I started to write this piece, the TV screen was showing bombs falling on Baghdad and other cities in Iraq in a "shock and awe" campaign that some Muslims view as a war on Islam by new crusaders. Unfortunately, most Americans do not know that the former Vice-President of Iraq, Tariq Aziz, is a Christian and that the former President and number-one villain, Saddam Hussein, is a secular Muslim (if there is such a thing). He had gassed and killed thousands of fellow Muslims. Thus, this war was not as simple as some people may believe.

Sister Meg, as I call her, has much in common with me in addition to sharing One God. We have lived in the same town in the United States for several decades; we belong to the same interfaith movement and are dedicated to Muslim–Catholic dialogue. We are for peace and against war. She is both more saintly and more "normal" than I. ("Normal" is a term she uses for good Muslims.) We admire each other and communicate through e-mail on a weekly basis. She calls me her brother and I call her my sister. We rarely see each other more than once a year. She is busy as a nun and I am busy as a physician. She invites people to God and I take care of God's creations. After the tragedy of September 11, 2001, a few hate-mongers sent me hate-email and a bomb threat. Sister Meg sent me a rose and a prayer of support.

Even though I believe that only those who live in a religion should speak for that religion, I see nothing wrong with anyone trying to understand and appreciate the theology of others and sharing it with those whose only source of education is television and print media. I especially support such attempts if they have a positive effect in removing some prevailing misconceptions and bring people of faith closer to each other for the love of a common God and loving service to fellow human beings, irrespective of their professed or assigned faith. In a lecture I gave recently at an international Sufi convention, I said that people of faith are like mountain climbers, trying to reach the same peak from different directions. I called us an army of God, wearing different uniforms but marching toward the same God—not a fighting army but a salvation army, in service to fellow humans.

Sister Meg's book on Islam comes at a time when, after the tragedy of September 11, there has been a wave of Islamophobia in the media, supported by Christian evangelists. The Reverend Pat Robertson called Islam "the enemy," the Reverend Franklin Graham said Islam was "evil," the Reverend Jerry Falwell called the Prophet

Muhammad a "terrorist" and the Qur'an "worse than *Mein Kampf.*" The Reverend Jerry Vine from Florida called the Prophet Muhammad a "demon possessed" and a "pedophile." Sister Meg, however, calls Islam a jewel of religions and has high praise for the Prophet Muhammad as the last prophet. What a contrast of opinion among Christians! Meg is the kind of Christian that the Qur'an talks about when it says, "nearest in love, Muslims will find those who call themselves Christians, as among them are those who are dedicated to learning, those who have renounced the material world [monastics], and those who are not arrogant" (Qur'an 5:32).

I will mention some of my specific comments regarding the content of the book as a Muslim. I write this not to oppose or correct Meg's views, but to clarify Islam's correct position on these views as I see them.

I disagree with Meg's proposition that religion is crafted by humans. We Muslims believe that religion is inborn. The Qur'an states that when souls were created, God took a pledge from them that they would worship no God except one God or Allah, in Arabic *Ilahikumwahid* ("our Lord is one"). This is also the first commandment in the Bible, "Thou shall take no partners to God." Thus, the Prophet Muhammad said "children are born Muslim [submitting to the will of God] but it is the parents who make them Jews and Christians and people of other faiths." Thus, I believe that all humans are believers, as religion was built into them at the time of creation. Man is always in search of God.

Those who cannot find God create their own god in the form of Marx, Lenin or Stalin. Or they become their own god, worshiping materialism and themselves.

The second question one may ask is, "Why were different prophets sent? Wasn't Abraham alone enough?" The problem in this question is that humans rejected prophets during their lifetimes and persecuted them. They even killed some of them. Those who believed either forgot the teachings of their prophets after their death or tried to distort them. Therefore, we Muslims believe that Islam is not a new religion, but it is the continuum of the same religion that was revealed to Adam and to prophets through Jesus. The Prophet Muhammad described himself like a beautiful building, where people had noticed a missing block. If this block was installed, they said, it would be complete. The Prophet Muhammad said, "I am that missing block."

We Muslims believe that Muhammad was foretold in the Bible and that Jesus knew about the coming of another prophet. For example, in John 14:16, New International Version, Jesus says, "And I will ask the Father, and he will give you another Counselor to be with you forever." And in Deuteronomy 18:18 it is mentioned, "I will raise up for them a prophet like you [Moses] from among their brothers; I will put my words in his mouth, and he will tell them everything I command him."

Muslims also believe that the events of the first revelation to Muhammad, described by Meg, were documented in the Bible as well. Isaiah 29:12 says, "Or if you give the scroll to someone who cannot read, and say, 'Read this, please,' he will answer, 'I don't know how to read.' "

I would also like to speak briefly about the status of Jesus and Mary in Islam. They are key to the unity of Christians and Muslims. We Muslims love both of them and hold them in a very high position in our hearts. The miraculous conception and birth of Jesus is well described in the Qur'an Chapter 19, the chapter of Mary. We Muslims believe that Jesus was born without a father as a sign from God. The Qur'an says that "the likeliness in the creation of Jesus is in the creation of Adam. He created him out of dust and then He said unto him, 'Be and he is' "(3:59). I jokingly say to my audiences sometimes that God at least had one ingredient (i.e., a mother), in the creation of Jesus, while in the creation of Adam he had neither a mother nor a father. We Muslims believe that Jesus had many miracles given to him by God to establish him as a prophet, which include the healing of the blind and the leper, reviving the dead and making a bird out of clay. We believe he did not die on the cross but was raised into the heavens to be with God. Christians do not know that we Muslims do not wait for Muhammad or Moses to return but for Jesus to come back.

Sister Meg describes beautifully her understanding of the pillars of faith in Islam—belief, prayer, fasting, charity and pilgrimage—without having to perform all these rituals herself! Readers should know that no building is composed of pillars only. It needs a floor, roof, walls,

windows etc. These structures are the moral codes of
Islam—virtues such as honesty, truthfulness, respect for
parents and elders, kindness to neighbors, love and friendship. These values are common to all religions, but are I
believe especially shared by Islam and Christianity. I
would like to offer some specific comments about the
pillars.

Prayers: The formal prayers that are conducted five
times a day are called *salaat*. They are acts of communica-
tion to God, not just asking God for our needs. I am
frequently asked why Muslims pray five times a day. This
is because between prayers, worldly attractions, instigated
by Satan, divert us from remembrance of God. Thus, we
Muslims forget to practice the "presence of God" as Christians call it. In other words, the train of God-consciousness
that derails must return to the track. We are closest to God
when our forehead is touching the ground in prostration.
Muslims make the claim that they invented Islamic prayer,
but the fact is that it is the original prayer described in the
Bible for all believers. It is mentioned in Nehemiah 8:6:
"Ezra praised the Lord, the great God; and all the people
lifted their hands and responded, 'Amen! Amen!' Then
they bowed down and worshiped the Lord with their faces
to the ground." Regarding Islamic prayer, another question
that I get asked is why women have to pray behind men
instead of in front of them or side by side. This is because
our focus of attention must be God and nothing else. We

do not pray behind any photographs or statues, either. However, within a house, a husband and wife can pray side by side.

Zakat or charity is the right of the poor over the wealth of the rich. Our modern tax system for welfare did not exist in the year 570 CE but evolved out of the *zakat* system developed by Islam.

Fasting in Ramadan is not new to Islam. It was prescribed by God to all religions in some form to clean the body and soul. It is a form of learning and practicing self-restraint. As a physician, I can testify that it has many medical benefits.

Hajj, the pilgrimage to Mecca, is not like a Disney World tour. It combines all the rituals of Islam in the tradition of Abraham. Having just returned from my second *hajj* to renew my faith, I cannot fully describe the beauty, joy and experience it offers. A Muslim is reborn as sinless after performing a correct *hajj* and considers it as a great honor to be called by God to visit His first house, which we believe was built by Adam. The *hajj* is something to be experienced rather than described. How the *hajj* changes a person's spiritual growth, manifested in his external behavior, is best described by Malcolm X in his conversion from a hateful Muslim to a practicing true Muslim after performing his *hajj*.

Finally, a word about terrorism. Islam teaches the sanctity of life. Both in the Qur'an and in the Torah, it is mentioned that "if one kills one person, it is as if he has killed all of mankind." However, terrorism is a plague that now affects people of all faiths and of no faith. Sometimes terrorism is intended by people to defame a faith. Sister Meg mentioned the example of Algerian monks killed by Muslim terrorists. To my knowledge, these monks were killed not by Muslims, but by the secular Algerian Army to defame the Islamic democratic movement in that country. Not only individuals but the state as well can commit terror. Muslims, Christians and people of other faiths must join hands to eradicate this disease from the hearts of hate-mongers by learning to love one other, and especially our "enemy"—as Jesus taught us in his Sermon on the Mount (Matthew 5:43–48).

I believe this book will open the minds and eyes of the author's fellow Christians to Islam, and Muslims will say of Sister Meg, "I wish she was a Muslim." Maybe she is and she does not know it.

Dr. Shahid Athar is a physician who has practiced endocrinology at St. Vincent Hospital, Indianapolis since 1974. He is also on the clinical faculty at Indiana University School of Medicine. He is a Fellow, American College of Physicians and American College of Endocrinology and a volunteer Clinical Associate Professor of Medicine at Indiana University School of Medicine in Indianapolis. Dr. Athar has written and published over 120 articles on Islamic topics and has spoken to many institutions and written for many publications throughout the United States. He is a regular contributor to *The Indianapolis Star* and serves on the editorial board of *Islamic Horizon* and *Muslim Voice*. Dr.

Athar has been involved with Christian and Muslims for Peace, Amnesty International, Physicians for Human Rights, Islamic Medical Association in North America, and others. He is a United States citizen and lives in Indianapolis with his wife and four children. His most recent books are *Reflections of an American Muslim*, *Health Concerns for Believers* and *Sex Education: An Islamic Perspective* all published by Kazi Publications, Chicago. His books can be accessed on the Internet at www.islam-usa.com.

A Select Bibliography
on God-consciousness

This bibliography was compiled by Mary Margaret Funk and Colleen Mathews. These books are more samples than a comprehensive survey. We focused on finding sources so that others could explore the amazing tradition of God-consciousness in Islam, Christianity, Hinduism, Judaism, and limited ourselves to books.

As we worked, however, it became time for Vespers on the Feast of St. Bernard, and we looked up at the same moment and glanced at each other. We concluded simultaneously that books were a start, but that the burden of the story should be shared through art, music, poetry, drama, sculpture and photography. God-consciousness in Islam was communicated to Meg not through our shared papers and background reading but by praying together at the Plainfield mosque and the hours around the table of dialogue. Colleen's love for Jewish mysticism emerged out of her years of *lectio divina* of the Hebrew scriptures. Meg's affinity for Hindu God-consciousness was a fruit of five years of study with Lalitha Krishnan, who was indeed God-conscious.

In working with East–West dialogue, Monastic Interreligious Dialogue (MID) has sponsored dialogues on
emerging topics. In 2000, MID gathered Christians and
Hindus for a dialogue on God-consciousness. The aim is to
publish the papers by 2004 on our Web site: monasticdi-
alog.com. These papers take the points of entry into Christ-
consciousness and expand on them. This, we feel, is an ongoing dialogue.

In 1999, we gathered in Schuyler, Nebraska for a
meeting on Christ in the 21st Century. The papers from the
Contact Persons Workshop on God-consciousness were
published in the May 2000 edition of the Monastic Interreligious Dialogue Bulletin, Issue #64, with James
Wiseman as the editor. This edition archives dialogue
about Christ-consciousness with the wisdom of Ewert
Cousins of Fordham University; Sean O'Duinn, OSB, of
Glenstal Abbey, Ireland; Swami Nityananda Giri of India
and Dr. Bettina Bäumer of the Abhishiktananda Society of
India. This conference was MID's most serious attempt at
dialogue on the topic of Christ-consciousness and promo-
tion of the process of dialogue as a means to Christ-
consciousness among believers.

We hope this little book will awaken the readers' own
God-consciousness from their own tradition and help them
benefit from other traditions as well. We believe this brief
list will be a helpful start, and we encourage readers to shift
to forms of music, poetry and the visual arts for more of
the "spirit."

Christianity

Abhishiktananda. *Prayer.* New ed. (Delhi: ISPCK, 1993).
Written by a French Benedictine who became a *sannyasa* in India, this book is his classic teaching to help the disciple to find the inward path of awakening to God.

———. *The Secret of Arunachala: A Christian Hermit on Shiva's Holy Mountain.* Rev. ed. (Delhi: ISPCK, 1997).
The biography describes how Abhishiktananda took a solo journey East. While living as a hermit on the sacred mountain of Arunachala in India he experienced the non-dual Presence emerging from the depths of his consciousness.

Alfeyev, Hilarion. *The Mystery of Faith: An Introduction to the Teaching and Spirituality of the Orthodox Church.* Ed. Jessica Rose. (London: Darton, Longman, and Todd, 2002).
A personal commentary by an Orthodox priest on the teachings of the Orthodox Church and their relationship to the practice of the spiritual life.

The Art of Prayer: An Orthodox Anthology. Comp. Igumen Chariton of Valamo. Trans. E. Kadloubovsky and E. M. Palmer. Ed. Timothy Ware. (London: Faber and Faber, 1966).
Texts on prayer and watchfulness of thoughts drawn from Greek and Russian sources. Also featured are texts on the Jesus Prayer, which becomes the Prayer of the Heart.

Barnhart, Bruno. "Christian Self-Understanding in the Light of the East: New Birth and Unitive Consciousness," in *Purity of Heart and Contemplation: A Monastic Dialogue between Christian and Asian Traditions.* Ed. Bruno Barnhart and Joseph Wong. (New York: Continuum, 2001).
A teaching from the Christian tradition on Unitive Consciousness.

Bossis, Gabrielle. *He and I.* Trans. Evelyn M. Brown. (Sherbrooke, Que.: Editions Mediaspaul, 1985).

Fragments of Gabrielle's conversations with Jesus in which she is taught to speak, think and be with her Lord. This is an example of colloquy that begins with self-talk and evolves into Christ-consciousness.

Brother Lawrence of the Resurrection. *The Practice of the Presence of God.* Trans. Robert J. Edmonson. Ed. Hal M. Helms. (Brewster, Mass.: Paraclete Press, 1985).

Teachings on the practice of a vivid recollection of God in the imagination or understanding. The practitioner shifts from remembering God to an experience through God's grace of God's abiding Presence.

Cassian, John. *The Conferences.* Trans. Boniface Ramsey. Ancient Christian Writers. (New York: Paulist Press, 1997).

Cassian's *Conferences* are a collection of teachings from the early Desert Fathers. There is no clearer teaching on pure interior prayer in the Christian tradition than Abba Isaac's conferences 9 and 10. John Cassian through the lips of Abba Isaac demonstrates the link between practice and prayer.

The Cloud of Unknowing and the Book of Privy Counseling. Ed. William Johnston. (New York: Image, 1973).

This spiritual classic from fourteenth-century England teaches the practice of lifting the heart to the Lord with love, centering all attention on him and forgetting all else.

De Caussade, Jean Pierre. *Abandonment to Divine Providence.* Trans. John Beevers. (Garden City, N.Y.: Image Books, 1975).

The essence of the teaching of de Caussade is that God is in the present moment and that each moment manifests God's will and design for our lives. The practice is to bring the mind's eye to the duty, the sacrament of the present moment, and abandon all else as illusion.

De Waal, Esther. *The Celtic Way of Prayer.* (New York: Doubleday, 1997).

Presents the riches of Celtic spirituality in the prayers, poems and liturgy of Celtic Christians that sprang from a natural consciousness of God present in the world about them.

Gregory of Nyssa. *The Life of Moses.* Trans. Abraham J. Malherbe and Everett Ferguson. Classics of Western Spirituality. (New York: Paulist Press 1978).

An account of the soul's ascent to God in the darkness of unknowing.

McGinn, Bernard. "Gregory the Great: The Contemplative in Action," in *The Growth of Mysticism,* vol. 2. (New York: Crossroad, 1994), pp. 34–79.

Reviews Gregory the Great's spiritual teaching on the Christian path to the contemplative vision of God that is attainable in this life.

Merton, Thomas. *The New Man.* 1961. (New York: Farrar, Straus and Giroux, 1999).

In this book of meditations Merton reflects on the theme of spiritual identity, saying that this identity will be found not in self-consciousness but God-consciousness.

——. *When the Trees Say Nothing: Writings on Nature.* Ed. Kathleen Deignan. (Notre Dame, Ind.: Sorin Books, 2003).

God-consciousness springs up when we are in the presence of nature. Kathleen, with the keen eye of a ritual artist, gathers Thomas Merton's poetic prose on nature.

Palamas, Gregory. *The Triads*. Trans. Nicholas Gendle. Classics of Western Spirituality. (New York: Paulist Press, 1983).

> The writings of Gregory Palamas epitomize the Orthodox Church's teaching on deification of humanity, both body and soul.

Theophan the Recluse. *The Path to Salvation: A Manual of Spiritual Transformation*. Trans. Seraphim Rose. (Forestville, Calif.: St. Herman of Alaska Brotherhood, 1996).

> This nineteenth-century interpretation of the ancient wisdom of the Christian East contains precise instructions on the spiritual life.

The Way of a Pilgrim and the Pilgrim Continues His Way. 1965. Trans. R. M. French. (San Francisco: Harper Collins. 1991).

> The story of a nineteenth-century Russian pilgrim who seeks to "pray without ceasing" through the practice of the Jesus Prayer.

Van Kaam, Adrian and Susan Muto. *The Power of Appreciation. A New Approach to Relational and Emotional Healing*. (Pittsburgh, PA: Epiphany Association. 1993).

> Formative Spirituality, of which this is one of over 100 books by Father van Kaam and Dr. Susan Muto, has at its center "The Mystery." This scientific approach to spirituality has a congruent anthropology, theology and psychology. The training is accompanied by a metalanguage for intelligibility that gives "form" to one's contemporary spirituality no matter what tradition is sourced. God-consciousness rises when neuroforms are transformed. Appreciation become "awe" in an abiding disposition.

Hinduism

The Bhagavad Gita: A New Translation and Commentary, 2 volumes. Trans. Paramahansa Yogananda. (Los Angeles: Self-Realization Fellowship, 1995).

This detailed commentary is an elucidation of the classic *Bhagavad Gita* that brings the creator and creature into realization of one consciousness. This epic scripture is considered a transmission of God-consciousness in the Hindu tradition.

Bhaskarananda, Swami. *The Essentials of Hinduism: A Comprehensive Overview of the World's Oldest Religion.* (Seattle: Viveka Press, 1994).

An excellent, readable first book on Hinduism that gives a graspable "sense" of the faith. Illustrations, suggested reading list, glossary, festivals, for reference. The God-consciousness or bliss is experienced after liberation is achieved by sincere spiritual practice.

Lennoy, Richard. *Anandamayi: Her Life and Wisdom.* (Rockport, Mass.: Element, 1996).

"There is only One and there is nothing outside of Him.... Man is a human being only inasmuch as he aspires to Self-realization." Anandamayi is an example of a guru who was God-conscious in her earthly life.

Ramana, Maharshi. *The Spiritual Teaching of Ramana Maharshi.* (Boston: Shambhala, 1988).

The Master guru who transmitted God-consciousness through silence and very few words but has a method, if it's used by God's invitation, that shifts from inquiry to realization of God-consciousness.

Yatiswarananda, Swami. *Meditation and Spiritual Life.* Revised edition. (Bangalore: Ramakrishna Math, 1983).

A readable textbook that gives a Westerner a full teaching on Indian spirituality with breadth and depth. It takes practices and shows how they are connected with spiritual experience of God-consciousness.

Islam

Armstrong, Karen. *Islam: A Short History.* Rev. ed. (New York: Modern Library, 2002).

This readable story of Islam as a culture also shows how the particular revelation of Allah that started with Muhammad became the God-consciousness of a people.

——. *Muhammad: A Biography of the Prophet.* (San Francisco: Harper Collins, 1992).

To understand Islam is to share in the same God-consciousness that Muhammad the Prophet had.

Athar, Shahid. *Reflections of an American Muslim.* (Chicago: Kazi Publications, 1994).

As a God-conscious man himself, Dr. Athar shares a view of Islam that shifts ethical behavior from being good to being in God.

Ernst, Carl W. *The Shambhala Guide to Sufism.* (Boston: Shambhala, 1997).

The Sufi tradition is the mystical manifestation of Islam.

Goodwin, Rufus. "Prayer Rugs: Islamic Tradition," in *Give Us This Day: The Story of Prayer.* (Hudson, N.Y.: Lindisfarne Books, 1999).

Through practice, God-consciousness not only rises during prayer but is sustained through ordinary time in everyday consciousness.

Hathout, Hassan. *Reading the Muslim Mind*. (Burr Ridge, Ill: American Trust Publications, 1995).

> The experience of God-consciousness that is in all our theistic religions has a particular manifestation with Muslims, to be respected by outsiders.

Kaltner, John. *What Non-Muslims Should Know*. (Minneapolis: Fortress Press, 2003).

> One thing to know about Islam is that the consciousness of God is of the same God of the Jews, Christians and Hindus.

The Meaning of the Glorious Koran: An Explanatory Translation. Trans. Mohammed Marmaduke Pickthall. (Multan, Pakistan: Maktaba Jawahar al Uloom, n.d.).

> The most sacred text that transmits God-consciousness.

Tweedie, Irina. *The Chasm of Fire*. 1979. (Rockport, Mass.: Element, 1993).

> The detailed journey of Irina Tweedie, a former atheist who undergoes training under a Sufi sheikh into the highest levels of God-consciousness.

Judaism

Buber, Martin. *Hasidism and Modern Man*. 1958. Ed. and trans. Maurice Freedman. (Amherst: Humanity Books, 1988).

> A classic collection of six meditations interpreting the Hasidic way of living in the continuous presence of God.

Buxbaum, Yitzhak. *Jewish Spiritual Practices*. (Northvale, N.J.: Aronson, 1990).

> A comprehensive guidebook to the wealth of Jewish spiritual practices whose goal is the attainment of God-consciousness.

Halevi, Klein Yossi. *At the Entrance to the Garden of Eden: A Jew's Search for God with Christians and Muslims in the Holy Land.* (New York: Harper Collins, 2001).

A moving account of an Israeli Jew's desire to find common ground with Muslims and Christians in prayer and other spiritual practices.

Heschel, Abraham Joshua. *I Asked for Wonder: A Spiritual Anthology.* Ed. Samuel H. Dresner. (New York: Crossroad, 1996).

This anthology of Heschel's work reflects the life of a man descended from Hasidic rabbis who experienced the presence and power of the living God.

Kaplan, Aryeh. *Jewish Meditation: A Practical Guide.* (New York: Schocken, 1985).

The teachings in this book were developed from the author's experience of translating the traditional teachings of Jewish meditation into practice for today.

Kushner, Lawrence. *Jewish Spirituality: A Brief Introduction for Christians.* (Woodstock, Vt.: Jewish Lights, 2001).

A review of key elements of Jewish spirituality, including the presence of God in everyday life, the Torah as a blueprint for creation and the commandments as sacred deeds which repair the world.

Martin Buber's Ten Rungs: Collected Hasidic Sayings. 1947. Ed. Martin Buber. (New York: Citadel Press, 1995).

Hasidic sayings that help us to see that love for God leads to love for others as we live out our day-to-day lives.

Meditation from the Heart of Judaism: Today's Teachers Share Their Practices, Techniques and Faith. Ed. Avram Davis. (Woodstock, Vt.: Jewish Lights Publishing, 1997).

Twenty-two contemporary guides give teachings and reflections on Jewish meditation as a practice that gives direct access to the Divine.

Pies, Ronald W. *The Ethics of the Sages: An Interfaith Commentary on the Pirkei Avot.* (Northvale, N.J.: Aronson, 2000).

Pirkei Avot is a rabbinic collection of ethical principles and rules for life that have been used by Jews for centuries as a guide to daily living. This commentary contains an analysis of the teachings contained in the *Pirkei Avot* in relation to similar or parallel teachings from Christianity, Buddhism, Islam, Hinduism and other spiritual traditions.

Steinsaltz, Adin. *The Thirteen Petalled Rose.* Trans. Yehuda Hanegbi. (Northvale, N.J.: Aronson, 1997).

A readable introduction to Jewish mystical thought by a distinguished scholar of the Talmud.

Verman, Mark. *The History and Varieties of Jewish Meditation.* (Northvale, N.J.: Aronson, 1996).

An expansive historical overview of Jewish meditative practices and their literary sources.

A Select Bibliography on Buddhist–Christian Dialogue

Buddhists Talk about Jesus, Christians Talk about the Buddha. Ed. Rita Gross and Terry Muck. (New York: Continuum, 2000). Interreligious dialogue on the two central figures of two major world faiths.

Christians Talk about Buddhist Meditation, Buddhists Talk about Christian Prayer. Ed. Rita Gross and Terry Muck. (New York: Continuum, 2003).
How meditation and prayer differ from one another and how they share some common themes.

Dalai Lama, His Holiness. *Spiritual Advice for Buddhists and Christians.* (New York: Continuum, 1998).
How to live a rich, contemplative life and cultivate oneself through meditation and prayer.

The Gethsemani Encounter: A Dialogue on the Spiritual Life by Buddhist and Christian Monastics. Ed. Donald W. Mitchell and James Wiseman. (New York: Continuum, 1997).
Reflections on Buddhist–Christian interreligious dialogue and the spiritual life from attendees at the first Gethsemani Encounter.

Fisher, Norman. *Opening to You: Zen-inspired Translations of the Psalms.* (New York: Viking Penguin, 2002).

A Buddhist monastic reimagines the Psalms from a Zen Buddhist perspective.

Fisher, Norman, Yifa, Judith Simmer-Brown, and Joseph Goldstein. *Benedict's Dharma: Buddhists Reflect on the Rule of St. Benedict.* (New York: Riverhead, 2001).

Four Buddhist monastics examine the impact of St. Benedict's rule on their own Buddhist spirituality.

Kennedy, Robert E. *Zen Spirit, Christian Spirit: The Place of Zen in Christian Life.* (New York: Continuum, 1996).

A Jesuit priest and Zen *sensei* reveals the common modes of reverence and self-examination between the Zen Buddhist and Christian traditions.

Purity of Heart and Contemplation: A Monastic Dialogue between Christian and Asian Traditions. Ed. Joseph Wong and Bruno Barnhart. (New York: Continuum, 2002).

Explorations of not only Buddhist–Christian dialogue, but also Taoist–Christian and Confucian–Christian, gathered from a conference at New Camaldoli Hermitage in Big Sur, California.

Transforming Suffering: Reflections on Finding Peace in Troubled Times. Ed. Donald W. Mitchell and James Wiseman (New York: Doubleday, 2003).

Thoughts on suffering from Buddhist and Christian monastics from the second Gethsemani Encounter.

Yifa. *Safeguarding the Heart: A Buddhist Response to Suffering and September 11.* (New York: Lantern Books, 2002).

A Chinese Buddhist nun examines the fundamental principles of Buddhism in the light of the terrorist attacks of September 11, 2001.